Andrew Bryson's Ordeal
An Epilogue to the 1798 Rebellion

IRISH NARRATIVES

IRISH NARRATIVES

Series edited by David Fitzpatrick

Personal narratives of past lives are essential for understanding any field of history. They provide unrivalled insight into the day-to-day consequences of political, social, economic or cultural relationships. Memoirs, diaries and personal letters, whether by public figures or obscure witnesses of historical events, will often captivate the general reader as well as engrossing the specialist. Yet the vast majority of such narratives are preserved only among the manuscripts or rarities in libraries and archives scattered over the globe. The aim of this series of brief yet scholarly editions is to make available a wide range of narratives concerning Ireland and the Irish over the last four centuries. All documents, or sets of documents, are edited and introduced by specialist scholars, who guide the reader through the world in which the text was created. The chosen texts are faithfully transcribed, the biographical and local background explored, and the documents set in historical context. This series will prove invaluable for university and school teachers, providing superb material for essays and textual analysis in class. Above all, it offers a novel opportunity for readers interested in Irish history to discover fresh and exciting sources of personal testimony.

Other titles in the series:

Henry Stratford Persse's Letters from Galway to America, 1821–1832, edited by James L. Pethica and James C. Roy
Frank Henderson's Easter Rising, edited by Michael Hopkinson
Memoirs of Joseph Prost: A Redemptorist Missionary in Ireland, 1851–1854, translated and edited by Emmet Larkin and Herman Freudenberger

Forthcoming titles:

A Patriot Priest: A Life of Reverend James Coigly, edited by Dáire Keogh
'My Darling Danny': Letters from Mary O'Connell to her son Daniel, 1830–1832, edited by Erin Bishop

David Fitzpatrick teaches history at Trinity College, Dublin. His books include *Politics and Irish Life, 1913–1921* (1977) and *Oceans of Consolation: Personal Accounts of Irish Migration to Australia* (1995).

Andrew Bryson's Ordeal
An Epilogue to the 1798 Rebellion

Edited by
Michael Durey

CORK UNIVERSITY PRESS

In Memoriam
Shaun Patrick Ellesmere
1944–1991

First published in 1998 by
Cork University Press
Cork
Ireland

© Cork University Press 1998

British Library Cataloguing in Publication Data

A CIP catalogue record for this book is available from the British Library.

ISBN 1 85918 144 9

Typesetting by Red Barn Publishing, Skeagh, Skibbereen

Printed in Ireland by ColourBooks, Baldoyle, Co. Dublin

Contents

Acknowledgements

A copy of Andrew Bryson's narrative account of his experiences as a rebel and reluctant redcoat is in the Public Record Office of Northern Ireland (T1373). It is a copy of this document that I used in preparing the manuscript for publication. I gratefully acknowledge the Deputy Keeper of the Records' permission to publish this document. Ultimate copyright, and the original narrative, remains in the hands of the Robb family, the direct descendants of Nelly Robb (*née* Bryson), the recipient of Bryson's long letter. A copy of the document was given to the Public Record Office of Northern Ireland in the 1960s by Dr John C. Robb, whose son, John Daniel Robb, has given me permission to publish this version. I am most grateful to him for allowing me to do so and for the help he has given me — including checking my transcription against one made earlier in this century.

I also wish to thank Joan Phillipson, of Historical Research Associates, who for several years acted on, with good cheer and great efficiency, a barrage of requests from me regarding many Ulstermen, including Bryson, whose radicalism led them into exile across the Atlantic. Staff at the New York Public Library and the New York Historical Society also kindly helped me with my unfortunately unavailing attempts to discover Bryson's ultimate fate.

As a rebel who eventually settled in the United States, Bryson was one of a large number of Irish rebel exiles about whom I have written a book, *Transatlantic Radicals*, the culmination of a research project which was generously funded by the Australian Research Council. I am grateful for their financial assistance.

Introduction

Towards the end of his long narrative account of his sufferings, first as a rebel prisoner in 1798 and then as an unwilling recruit in the British army overseas, Andrew Bryson Jr appealed to his sister:

> Not to Expose the writer by letting any person See it Through Mottives of Curiousity, as It was not wrote to Gratify any Such person, but to Shew you how Great things God Has done for me in first preserving my life amids Sour according Death, & Afterwards in his own Good time & by the means which he thought best, Delivering me from the hands of mine Enemies. For which & for all his other mercies I know you will Redily Join with me in ascribing to a three [in] One God all praise, honour & Glory, world without End, Amen.

Whether Bryson's sister, Nelly (Mrs Daniel Robb of Ballysallagh), showed the narrative to others is not known, but after nearly two hundred years it may be agreed that 'Mottives of Curiousity' no longer have the capacity to expose Bryson's sufferings to the taunts of his political enemies or to the morbid sympathy of his friends. On the other hand, however, it is unlikely that with the re-emergence of Bryson's narrative curiosity will remain confined merely to the historian's purpose of 'Figuring the nature of the times deceas'd'.[1] Bryson's narrative has the capacity to raise questions — to some uncomfortable, to some unconventional and to some unfashionable — about the contexts and heritages of contemporary Ireland, both north and south. For Andrew Bryson was both a United Irish rebel and a devout Presbyterian, a combination which, nearly two hundred years after he wrote his narrative, appears to be both inexplicable and bizarre. Yet in the 1790s, if not a decade later, it was, if not typical, at least unexceptional.

Andrew Bryson Jr was born in April 1779, the second son of Andrew Bryson and his wife Isabella (*née* Barr). He was the fourth of their eight children, the eldest being Nelly (1772–1857), the recipient of his 1801 narrative. Andrew Bryson Sr farmed land held on long lease

1

in Ballysallagh, County Down, the core of which had been bequeathed to him while he was still a minor. Although his property was not large, it was sufficient to give him 'a comfortable competence'. His two sons, however, were put to the leather trades, the elder son David as a currier, Andrew as an apprentice tanner.[2]

The Brysons were originally from Renfrewshire, settling in Down during a period of significant migration from south-west Scotland in the early seventeenth century. They were of staunch Presbyterian stock, intermarrying with families of similar background such as the Robbs and the Finlays. The Rev. Andrew Bryson — as the narrative informs us, the invocation of his name was sufficient to improve young Andrew's situation in Lisburn jail — was only one of three kinsmen who were Presbyterian ministers, the others being Rev. James — Andrew's uncle — and Rev. William — his father's cousin. James, who died in 1796, was orthodox in his theology; William was of the Arian 'New Light' persuasion.[3] Judging by Andrew Bryson's praise of a triune God to his sister, his family was orthodox.

Making up about one-third of the population of Ulster but only one-tenth of the population of Ireland, Presbyterians in the eighteenth century held an anomalous position in Irish society. Although less burdened by official discrimination than Roman Catholics under their penal laws, they nevertheless, at the beginning of the American war in 1775, still did not possess full civil rights. They were prohibited from participating fully in local politics by the Test Act, and the degree of religious toleration which was extended to them by the ruling Protestant Ascendancy served only to heighten a sense of persecution, making a mockery of the Presbyterians' growing wealth and economic significance stemming from their role in the burgeoning linen industry.[4]

Unsurprisingly, when conflict with America in 1775 expanded into a war with France, Spain and Holland, threatening invasion, midde-class Ulster Presbyterian families like the Brysons took advantage of the crisis, making up the solid core of support for political and religious reform in Ireland. Led by a rising middle class of merchants and entre-preneurs in Belfast and urged on by their ministers, Presbyterian communities poured into the Volunteer corps from 1778, using the emergency as a pretext for their demands for full civil rights and an independent Irish legislature under the Crown in Dublin. Skilfully manipulating the politics of threat, the patriotic Volunteers in arms initially had several successes, culminating in 1782 in the Rockingham ministry's reluctant acceptance of their demands for the ending of formal British control over the Irish legislature. The Dublin and Westminster parliaments were now seemingly of equal status.[5]

At this moment of triumph, however, the Volunteer movement split into two sections: those who were satisfied with their achievements, and those — a smaller number led in the north by Belfast Presbyterians — who continued to agitate for parliamentary reform and relief for Catholics. Attempts to intimidate the Dublin parliament to reform itself were unsuccessful. By 1785, following the failure of the Dungannon Convention to pass a motion supporting Catholic Emancipation, an issue which fatally divided the Ulster Presbyterian community, the radical Volunteer movement was moribund.

For five years reform politics in Ulster remained quiescent; not even the first stages of the French Revolution could inspire renewed efforts for change, although news of the fall of the Bastille was enthusiastically received in Ireland.[6] The first signs of a reinvigorated reform movement among the Volunteers came with the election in County Down in 1790, when many future Presbyterian rebels supported Robert Stewart, Lord Castlereagh, who spent a reputed £6,000 to win the seat in the Whig interest.[7] Castlereagh's campaign was a catalyst that impelled the radicals of 1784–85 again to consider a campaign for parliamentary reform and Catholic Emancipation.[8]

The initial seat of this radical reform movement was Ulster, more specifically Belfast, and its founders were primarily middle-class Presbyterians. Their vehicle was the Society of United Irishmen, created, with some assistance from Theobald Wolfe Tone, by a group of Belfast Volunteers headed by Samuel Neilson in October 1791. A month later a society with the same name was founded in Dublin, and by the end of the year some of the smaller communities in Antrim and Down had followed the lead of Belfast.[9] Elsewhere in Ulster United Irishmen wisely penetrated existing organisations such as masonic lodges and Volunteer companies to extend their influence, rather than attempting to establish societies of their own.[10]

With many ups and downs the Society of United Irishmen, in its constitutional phase, lasted until the spring of 1794. Its avowed programme was the same as that of the radical Volunteers: a radical reform of parliament and full civil and political rights for Catholics, to be achieved by legal and constitutional means. In reality, however, by opening lines of communication with the Defender movement[11] and with small artisan Jacobin clubs in Belfast, the radical former Volunteers flirted with revolutionary plans from an early stage. In response, the Irish government, faced with the example of revolutionary France, initiated a policy of repression of the United Irish clubs combined with conciliatory measures towards the Catholics, whom they, with some initial success, attempted to detach from the grasp of the radicals. By the spring of 1794 the open United Irish societies had been forced to close down, although Neilson's radical newspaper, the *Northern Star*, survived all attempts to suppress it.[12]

Most of the halfhearted, less militant Presbyterians, suspicious of Catholic pretensions, had left the movement by 1794, but Neilson and his group did not surrender. Rather, they began to link together the various forms of discontent in Ireland into one secret, highly structured and disciplined organisation, with political and military wings, ready to take advantage of any French invasion. This revamped United Irish secret society fed off the disappointment arising from the failure of Earl Fitzwilliam's short period as Lord Lieutenant of Ireland, when the hopes for parliamentary reform and Catholic Emancipation were finally and irrevocably dashed, and off the hostility inspired by the spread of the Orange Order from its beginnings in Armagh in 1795.[13]

The basic structure of the political wing of the underground United Irish society was cellular, with local societies splitting into two once thirty-six members had been reached. Above these, and deriving from them, were committees at the barony, county and provincial level. At the apex was a national committee.[14] The purpose of this system was to keep all plans on a 'need-to-know' basis (as far as was possible in a mass organisation; in practice, the structure was easily penetrated by spies and informers). Side by side with this political framework from 1796, and mirroring its structure, was a military system, based on platoons of ten or eleven men (one a sergeant), with ten platoons commanded by a captain. Within each barony the captains elected a colonel, while each county was under the control of an adjutant-general, chosen by the central leadership from a list of names provided by the county's colonels.[15] Andrew Bryson first came to government notice as a captain in this military system.

One of the major roles of the political wing was to turn the underground society into a national but secret movement. As early as May 1795 the government in Dublin Castle was receiving reports of night-time travellers being sent from Belfast to surrounding villages to administer oaths.[16] Later in the year the better-organised regions such as Ulster were circulating emissaries throughout the country, swearing the unhappy, the frightened and the disaffected into the organisation.[17] At the same time, vigorous attempts were made to suborn the military, especially the mainly Catholic militia. By late 1796, according to the informer Leonard McNally, the whole camp at Blaris Warren, near Lisburn, had been sworn into the United/Defender movement.[18]

For the whole of 1796 and the early months of 1797 the roving emissaries administered oaths with virtual impunity. A wave of fear — 'a reign of terror' one Castle correspondent from County Tyrone called it — swept the north and midlands of Ireland, reinforced by the intimidatory tactics of both sides.[19] Even when United Irishmen were arrested and tried in the criminal courts, they were frequently acquitted. Jury panels were too scared to convict; witnesses were bought off or quietly disappeared.[20]

Government responses to the loss of control in the disaffected regions and to the shrill complaints of the loyalists included the suspension of *habeas corpus* and the use of the Insurrection Act in Ulster (the act gave increased powers to magistrates in proclaimed areas).

Yeomanry corps were raised, mainly as a local force to allow the regular army and the militia to concentrate on defence against a French invasion, but they were swiftly penetrated by the Orange Order. Suspension of *habeas corpus* allowed the government to order the arrest in September 1796 of the most prominent Belfast leaders, including Neilson. They were all transferred to Dublin, where they remained incarcerated for many months, although never brought to trial.

Finally, in March 1797 the government ordered General Gerard Lake to disarm the north: 'The Authority is full and without limitation excepting which your own discretion may suggest.'[21] Lake was well suited to this task. Blessed neither with discretion nor sensitivity, his vigorous activities almost certainly prevented an insurrection in Ulster in the spring and summer of 1797. He roughly compelled the disaffected to disgorge their hidden arms, stolen in night raids, and he seized the gunpowder secretly supplied from Dublin and America in flax-seed casks.[22] He disrupted the county organisations by arresting many of the United Irish leaders and watched with equanimity as around the streets of Belfast zealous magistrates guided a masked spy, Edward Newell, to pick out men whom he had seen at secret United Irish meetings.[23]

One of the many caught in this dragnet was the eighteen-year-old Andrew Bryson's father, who was arrested by Lake under a warrant for treasonable practices in May 1797.[24] For seven months he endured captivity in Belfast, until in November he was one of twelve prisoners freed on bail after Thomas Addis Emmet and William Sampson — both prominent lawyers but also major United Irish leaders — successfully served a writ of *habeas corpus*.[25]

Whether Andrew Bryson Jr was already involved in the United Irish movement before his father's arrest cannot be ascertained, but by the time he definitely was the initiative had shifted from the Belfast to the Dublin leaders.[26] In Ulster many of those who had suffered periods of imprisonment lost their enthusiasm for the cause. Hundreds of others had been forced to flee abroad. Lake's policy had been brutal but effective. By the end of 1797 the United Irish movement in Ulster had suffered an almost fatal blow.[27]

One consequence was that in the months leading up to the rebellion — it broke out in Kildare on 24 May 1798 but not until a fortnight later in Antrim and Down — very young men like Bryson were thrust into the senior positions in the Ulster United Irish organisation. The arrest and flight of so many experienced leaders in 1797 partly explain their promotion, but also of significance was the irresolution, even cowardice, of some of the more mature leaders in Antrim and Down at the onset of the crisis in May 1798. It was not just that the two core positions of adjutants-general were vacant in June — Rev. William Steel Dickson of Down was arrested just hours before the insurrection, and Robert Simms of Antrim 'retired' at about the same time — but for many months previously there had been an air of defeatism and languor among the leaders in east Ulster. Youthful firebrands like Bryson, the eighteen-year-old Richard Caldwell and many young Presbyterian licentiates became the victims of the United Irishmen's escalator policy of filling vacant positions with the next in seniority.[28]

Bryson was part of the military wing of the United Irishmen. Initially he was a captain, commanding — in theory — one hundred men in the Newtownards area. But by 31 March 1798 he had been promoted to colonel and was a member of the County Down committee of colonels which met in his home town (but swiftly adjourned because of the proximity of a zealous magistrate).[29] Everything, however, was in confusion. At a meeting of the Ulster provincial committee in Armagh on 29 May, called to determine the province's response to news of the insurrection in the south, Thomas Bashford Jr, a Belfast shopkeeper, angrily denounced the Ulster Executive for having refused to prepare for rebellion. According to a report from the informer Nicholas Magin, Bashford 'thought they completely betrayed the People both of Leinster and Ulster, and he thought it the duty of the present Committee to denounce and vote them out of office, and to take some speedy and vigorous measures to second the efforts of the People in the Upper Provinces'.[30] Reluctantly, all but the Down delegates agreed to rise, although many believed that in the key counties of Antrim, Down and Armagh the organisation was too weak to disarm the local army units.[31]

The military wing was similarly divided. Colonels of ten regiments met at Saintfield on 31 May and were 'generally determined to act', but a day later only two of twenty-three colonels were prepared to rise without either a French invasion or proof of rebel success around Dublin.[32] Four days later the Down colonels were urging their adjutant-general to begin the rebellion. Such inconsistency was a recipe for disaster, which unfolded relentlessly over the next few weeks. The rebellion in east Ulster — the stronghold of the movement in the north — was to be too late, too tepid and too unorganised.

Among the young enthusiasts like Bryson, disillusionment came swiftly. Robert Adrain, a brilliant young tutor in mathematics and languages, was to be stabbed in the back by his own disaffected troops and left for dead, even before the British army had been sighted.[33] When the Down licentiate Colonel William Fox heard that Henry Joy McCracken was advancing on Antrim at the head of a rebel army, he climbed Scrabo Hill, near Newtownards, expecting to find his regiment awaiting orders. The hill was deserted. Looking down on the bustle in the barracks below, he realised that the element of surprise had been lost. The next day, learning that Saintfield was 'up', he urged his horse towards Bangor and Donaghadee, raising the country as he went. That night he led a section of the 300-strong rebel force to attack Newtownards, but they fled after blundering into another rebel column in the dark. By the time they had regrouped, the garrison had evacuated the town. Thereafter his little army was reluctant to move. 'I was torn by a thousand vexations', he later wrote from America, 'which no person but one who may have been in my situation can understand or feel — however, after much flattery, I got them to march off by companies and it was 11 o'clock [p.m.] before the rere marched off the hill' (into oblivion at the battle of Ballynahinch).[34]

It is unfortunate that there is no record of what Andrew Bryson was doing during these days of confusion and disappointment. The statement in his narrative, that on board ship for the West Indies he saw for the first time a person die, suggests that he could not have been in the thick of the fighting during the rebellion.[35] He may have remained in

Newtownards once the rebels had taken it without bloodshed. His father was implicated in 'the Traitorous Committee, who assumed full Powers and exercised . . . Civil and Military Jurisdiction, in the Town of N.T. Ards during the Rebellion'. Perhaps out of fatherly concern he ensured that his son was part of the guard that remained to destroy bridges, strengthen defences and supply provisions to the rebel forces massing at Ballynahinch?[36]

What is certain is that Andrew Bryson Jr went into hiding following the collapse of the rebellion. By late July his name was second on a list of 'Down Leaders and Principals' who had evaded capture and on whose heads a reward of £50 was to be offered.[37] He was subsequently among those who were named individually as being exempt from the provisions of an act of pardon (38 Geo. III, c. 55) and who were proclaimed under the Fugitive Act. Unless Bryson surrendered to the authorities before 1 December 1798, he was to be deemed guilty of high treason.[38]

Whether Bryson voluntarily surrendered or was captured is not now known, but with John Adams and James McCann he was brought to court martial some time in September 1798. His life was certainly in danger, for the authorities believed they had two witnesses whose evidence could convict him of a capital offence.[39] At their court martial all three rebels were found guilty and sentenced to enlist in a regular regiment of the British army for a period of years. When this sentence was reported to Lord Lieutenant Cornwallis, he objected to the limited length of service and the provision that the offenders could choose the regiment in which they would enlist. Cornwallis increased the sentence to general military service overseas for life.[40]

The records of Bryson's trial unfortunately no longer exist. Probably they were among the host of court-martial papers sent to the Lord Lieutenant that were subsequently filed among judicial records in the Four Courts and which were destroyed by fire during the civil war in 1922. It is thus almost impossible to determine whether Bryson was unlucky in having his sentence changed to general service overseas. Cornwallis's general policy towards the rebels was one of qualified leniency. He was

prepared to pardon the thousands of rank and file implicated in the
rebellion, once they had surrendered their arms and taken the oath of
allegiance.[41] He also commuted one-third of the court-martial capital
sentences that he reviewed in 1798.[42] Although less sympathetic to the
rebel leaders — among whom he included any officer above the rank of
captain in the military wing of the United Irishmen — Cornwallis
nevertheless permitted many of them to be banished. He was particularly generous towards young rebel leaders from Ulster, especially Presbyterian licentiates. With Castlereagh's support, he was always prepared
to be influenced by petitions for leniency from prominent local Protes-
tants and the families of young rebel leaders.[43]

In contrast to other young Ulster rebels, Bryson appears to have had
his sentence made more punitive by the Lord Lieutenant's intervention.
General military service overseas was not, in Cornwallis's view, the
severest non-capital punishment he could mete out — that was transportation to Botany Bay[44] — but enlistment in a regular regiment that
would not have to endure the unhealthiness of the West Indian climate
was considered to be of lesser severity. Not knowing the charge Bryson
faced (although it probably was the general offence of treason and
rebellion), it is difficult to determine why Cornwallis made the decision that he did, although one explanation is suggested by Bryson's narrative. Just before he left the prison ship in Belfast on his journey south,
Bryson was informed that his uncle's intervention had resulted in his
being forced overseas. Almost certainly this was a reference to his
father's cousin, Rev. William Bryson, who was a staunch loyalist in
1798.[45] Under Cornwallis's policy, failure to obtain the universal support of one's kin was fatal for any hope of being treated leniently. One
dissentient would have been sufficient to dash the hopes of his other relatives, although the role of his father in the rebellion may also have
reduced the impact of their petitioning. There seems little doubt that
William Bryson was instrumental in convincing the authorities that the
peace of Ireland would be buttressed by Andrew's permanent exile
overseas.

*

Bryson's narrative begins on the day before he, with twelve other prisoners, was taken ashore from the prison ship *Postlethwaite* lying in Belfast Lough, where he had been languishing since his trial three months earlier. Their ultimate destination in Ireland, once another ten or eleven convicts had been added to their number — many of whom were not United Irishmen, but either common criminals or deserters — was the new holding camp at New Geneva, near Waterford.[46] In late 1798 hundreds of prisoners were being herded towards this camp, the result of panic among government lawyers who feared that many court-martial verdicts determined in the aftermath of the rebellion would shortly be declared unsafe. In November the lawyers acting for Wolfe Tone at his trial for treason had asserted the illegality of courts martial held while the civil law remained operative.[47] Their argument was controversial, but government lawyers believed it stood a good chance of being accepted if brought before the civil magistrates (although it did not help Tone, who had committed suicide).[48] In an attempt to prevent rebel prisoners being freed on writs of *habeas corpus*, Lord Lieutenant Cornwallis ordered all prisoners currently being held in city and county jails, tenders and other places of confinement to be funnelled as quickly as possible to the giant military holding camp at New Geneva, from where, it was hoped, they could be swiftly sent overseas.[49] Bryson was thus only one of many dozens of Ulster rebels who were forced to march from their home province to County Waterford in the winter of 1798–99.

Bryson's narrative falls neatly into three sections: an account of his experiences as a prisoner in Ireland, from the time he left Belfast to the moment he boarded a troopship for overseas service; an account of the sea trip from Ireland to the West Indies; and an account of his travails on Martinique as a reluctant soldier, up to the point of his escape. In all three sections he makes significant contributions to an understanding of the aftermath of the Irish rebellion.

His detailed account of the march from Belfast to New Geneva is unique, for although hundreds of rebels made a similar march from their jails to the prison camp in 1798 and 1799, no other prisoner was able to leave such a sketch of his experiences. Bryson's detailed account of his privations on the journey, of the deplorable and overcrowded state of some of the prisons, of the petty tyrannies exercised primarily by his great foes — yeomen, Orangemen and Quakers — and of the small victories with which he and his compatriots kept up their morale, are of considerable importance for an understanding of the plight of rebel prisoners in this period. The equally small kindnesses which Bryson received, from ordinary Irish men and women, fellow rebel prisoners, a few jailers and even occasionally English army officers, also should be recognised as part of the wider story.

But perhaps of greatest value in the first section of his narrative is Bryson's description of life in New Geneva barracks, where he spent six weeks, for no other first-hand account exists of that temporary holding camp from the point of view of the prisoners. Yet many thousands of rebels (and ordinary criminals) were to be confined there in the next few years, some of whom were to be sent to Botany Bay and some to Prussia. Most, however, about 1,500 in number, were to follow in Bryson's footsteps to the West Indies. The camp had been established in a hurry, and although it was obviously of a much higher standard than most of the country's prisons, it was equally overcrowded — one effect of the government's inability to find suitable transports in this period.[50] As Bryson so graphically portrays, the camp was also subject to frequent escape attempts, a few of which were successful, the rest culminating in fearful punishments for those recaptured. The mood of determination and the camaraderie among the 'Northerns' which Bryson imparts is reminiscent of the accounts of prisoner-of-war camps in Germany during the Second World War. The reckless desire to escape is, indeed, a mood that pervades the whole of Bryson's captivity narrative.

The second part of Bryson's manuscript, a narration of the month-long journey by sea from Passage to Martinique, is also of significant value, for again, no other account exists, although at least three other convoys of Irish rebel 'soldiers' were to arrive in the West Indies over the next few years. Bryson describes the routine of life on board ship, the petty enmities that arise from so many living at close quarters for so long, the suspicions held by the military and naval authorities of the loyalty of the Irish recruits when the enemy was thought to be near, and, rather ruefully, the enthusiasm of some of his fellow prisoners at the prospect of gaining prize money. Above all, however, Bryson rewards us with an unexpectedly full account of a crossing-the-line ceremony, when for a short time the enclosed world of the ship was turned upside down. Capable of being interpreted in a number of ways — as simply a form of theatre or as a customary and acceptable form of extortion, for instance — the ceremony as portrayed by Bryson reflects the influence of a plebeian moral economy on the high seas, with two unpopular officers (the ship's purser and one of the prisoners' officers) undergoing humiliating and painful treatment by King Neptune's barber.[51] Significantly, however, the Irish recruits remained only passive witnesses to the ceremony, non-persons in this traditional world.

The one-month voyage for Bryson ended at Martinique, where, in an amelioration of their earlier sentence to general service, the Irish recruits were permitted a choice of regiment in which to enlist. Bryson and nine other 'Northerns' decided to remain on the island, among a complement of thirty-four who opted to join the 43rd Regiment. The rest sailed on to Jamaica. With Martinique now safely in the hands of the British, and no longer threatened by significant French forces in the West Indies, the role of the British army was confined to garrison duty. The third part of Bryson's narrative is concerned with his experiences as a member of this garrison in a beautiful but deadly open prison.

A nineteenth-century history of the 43rd Regiment, discussing its role in 1799, confines itself to one laconic sentence: 'The regiment remained at St Pierre, and suffered terribly from the pestiferous atmosphere.'[52] Not for nothing were the regiments stationed in the West Indies during the French war called the 'condemned regiments'. Throughout the 1790s epidemic fevers killed far more European troops than either bullet or bayonet. Yellow fever was epidemic, travelling with displaced planters as far as the eastern seaboard of the new United States. Other diseases, dysentery, relapsing and remittent fevers, also took their annual toll.[53] Bryson was to be afflicted within forty-eight hours of arrival on Martinique, first with what was diagnosed as heatstroke, then with a remittent fever which left him permanently weak and debilitated. Many of those who had disembarked with him soon died in the military hospital, the failings of which Bryson describes in ghastly detail (although the rough humanity of the doctor working in desperate conditions is also clearly apparent).

One continuing thread through the narrative is Bryson's determination to raise himself above his predicament. His cousin Samuel, a Glasgow medical student, wrote when he heard that Andrew had been sent to New Geneva: 'He now has nothing to do, but with Manly Resignation, to meet his fate. I know he *has the heart*, I hope he will be able to brave, nay to dare the worst.'[54] That Bryson justified his cousin's confidence is witnessed by his actions in captivity. Throughout his ordeal he conducted himself with fortitude and manliness remarkable in one so young. Undoubtedly his strong religious convictions helped sustain him; indeed, his narrative should be read as an honest, undramatic *confession* to his sister, rather than as a document prepared with an eye on posterity. (Internal evidence suggests that the letter, dated 28 May 1801, was not completed until 1804.)[55] Bryson, however, was also fortified by a sense of righteousness in the cause for which he was forced from his homeland. Direct political opinions are rarely expressed in the narrative — his comments on the imperial navigation laws and on the cruelty of slavery are exceptions — but Bryson's strong sense of pride and of his rights as a human being continually intrude in his relations with superior authority. He never allows himself to be browbeaten, nor does he avoid expressing his true convictions when he feels an injustice has been done. Only in the aftermath of his illness, the disappointment of missing an opportunity to escape from the island, and the news of the punishment of his friend Purse, is there evidence that his indomitable will to survive temporarily falters.

It is thus a major disappointment that his narrative ends before his escape, owing to his having explained it in a previous letter to his sister which cannot now be found. But it is clear from the narrative how his escape probably came about: a compliant American ship's captain would have assisted in his desertion. Desertion was, in fact, not uncommon: more than 3,000 cases were reported from the army in the West Indies between 1793 and 1801, including about 1,200 from the Windward and Leeward Islands.[56] Not all of them escaped from the islands, of course. Many of Bryson's fellow recruits fled into the mountains soon after arriving in Jamaica, where they joined up with Maroons and some remaining French troops to harass the British settlers.[57] Lethargy and boredom, the consequences of disease, the climate and routine garrison duties, must have reduced the ardour and watchfulness of the officers. A few, as is hinted at about one in the narrative, may even have sympathised with the plight of the younger, better-educated United Irishmen like Bryson, and while not turning a blind eye, nevertheless did not keep them under strict discipline. That Bryson and his friend Sibbett could take advantage of their opportunities says not only much for their perseverence and strength of will, but also something of the lassitude undermining army discipline in this theatre of operations.

It would be pleasant to be able to record that Bryson's ordeal had a happy ending, but unfortunately this cannot be done. The first portents were favourable. He probably arrived in the United States at the end of 1799 or the beginning of 1800 and would have found both his father and his brother David already settled in New York City.[58] There is no evidence that David had been involved in the rebellion, but Andrew Bryson Sr definitely was. He had not, however, been brought to trial, but was allowed voluntarily to banish himself. In October 1798 he had set out from Derry on the barque *Pallas* for America, but was driven back into Cork by violent storms. Orders were given for his arrest if he surfaced in Belfast, but he apparently found another ship in Cork to take him to America.[59]

In New York the Brysons established a family firm, probably in the grocery business.[60] They found themselves surrounded by dozens of fellow rebel exiles, some under life proscription, others who had fled in the face of arrest. Most, including the Brysons, experienced difficulty in settling into their new surroundings. They were unwilling immigrants, whose ties to Ireland remained strong.[61] At one point the Brysons contemplated emigrating *en masse* to America, but hopes that their exiled relatives might be allowed to return to Ireland were raised in 1806 after William Pitt died and the Whigs came to power in Britain.[62] The so-called Ministry of All the Talents relaxed the uncompromisingly tough line taken by the previous administration against the exiles, and a number of rebel leaders were permitted to return. Taking advantage of this window of opportunity, Andrew Bryson Sr returned to Ireland. But in September 1806 Charles James Fox, long sympathetic to the rebel exiles' cause, died, and the ministry did not long survive him, collapsing over the intractable problem of Catholic relief. Its replacement, headed by the elderly Duke of Portland, brought back to power many of the exiles' greatest foes, including Castlereagh. In these new circumstances, Bryson senior was informed that unless he quitted Ireland, he would be arrested.[63] He accordingly returned to the United States.

By this time Andrew Bryson Jr had once again slipped into the shadows. He was mentioned occasionally in surviving family letters, the last one dated March 1806. Unlike his brother, who played a role in the politics of the Irish community in New York, [64] Andrew proffered no public face. No mention of him can be found in any public documents in New York, nor in the city directories and newspapers of the time. He seems to have completely disappeared. The Robb–Bryson–Finlay family tree gives no information other than his date of birth. There is no record of his marrying, or of fathering children (in contrast to his brother, whose son Andrew became a rear-admiral in the US navy, having fought for the Union in the civil war).[65]

There are three possible explanations for the absence of further evidence on Bryson's life in the United States. The most unlikely one is that, like many other exiles,[66] he surreptitiously slipped back to Ireland, where he lived quietly and secretly. If that had happened, however, it almost certainly would have been recorded in subsequent family letters or memoirs. Second, he might have left New York for another part of the United States. But again, unless he had deliberately broken with his family, it is unlikely that his fate would have remained unknown by the descendants of the Brysons. The third explanation is thus the most likely: Bryson died prematurely in America at some point after 1806. Perhaps yellow fever finally caught up with him, for it continued to kill Americans along the eastern seaboard in the first decade of the century. Almost certainly he would never have fully recovered from the devastating impact that the cruel climate and vicious diseases of the West Indies had had on his health. His punishment for being a rebel finally took its full toll. The document produced here may be seen as his epitaph.

Editorial Note

I have intervened as little as possible while editing the text. I have where necessary introduced sentence and paragraph breaks, but have retained original spellings and capitalisations. Occasional obscurities in spelling etc. are clarified in italics within square brackets. Where Bryson is obviously using direct speech, and clarity is enhanced, I have added quotation marks. At points, tears in the manuscript and Bryson's untidy hand have made identification of words and phrases either difficult or impossible. Where the latter is the case, I have said so in italics within square brackets. Where I have hazarded a guess at a word or phrase, I have placed it, in roman type and followed by a question mark, within square brackets. Where the sense of what Bryson is trying to say is improved by an additional word, or where he has obviously missed out a word, I have included them, in roman type, within square brackets. I have also occasionally extended abbreviations, again also within square brackets.

Narrative of Andrew Bryson

in a letter to his sister, Nelly Robb, 28 May 1801

[PRONI, TI373]

New York May 28th 1801

My Dearest Sister

Having a few days before me in which I will not be very busily employed, I Sit down to endeavour to fullfill your request and my own promise of Giving you Some acc[t.] of my passage from Belfast to the West Indies, but as I had no Oppurtunitys of taking down the date of any occurances that happened [to] me, you need not expect that I can Give you an accurate acc[t.] of them. You are pretty well acquainted with what happened [to] me from the time that I went to Belfast untill the time that my Mother and Sisters came to See me on board the Prison-ship.[1] From that time till Christmas we spent our time in the usual way, Sometimes having reports in our favour and Sometimes against us.[2] The day before Christmas Mr. Gray made us a present of a Goose and at the Same time we received a present of Rum from Mr. Murrow, Lisburn and, being always in Good Spirits we prepared to have our Dinner in Stile, and not to be out of the fashion we resolved not to Dine till after Dark. You may remember that the[re] was a Small Shower that morn-ing. Of course we had foggy weather which prevented us from Seeing very far and Mr. Dickey[3] expecting Some people down to See him that evening, we were on the Look Out. Accordingly about three in the evening we perceived a boat and we were Soon all on Deck, Some expecting to See their friends and Some from Curiausity. As Soon as the boat came a Little nearer Mr. Gray told us that we might expect Company; indeed, for he was much mistaken if it was not one of the Guard boats coming with more prisoners. The words were not well out of his Mouth before there was another boat in Sight and in a few min-utes a third. It was now past Dispute and accordingly all hands went to work in order to have Dinner made for them and as there was plenty of fresh meat on board we had Soon as many ready as would have served all the people in the Prov[ost Prison]. In about half an hour after we first Saw them the first Boat came along side, in which was Mr. Teel-ing,[4] Dr. Dickson[5] and a very Great number of the most respectable

21

part of the prisoners. They were not Suffered to go below, however, till the other two boats came and the roll was called and then we all went down together and began to Dinner.[6]

The mess that I belonged to was only five in number and we had twenty to assist us in Eating Dinner and in Drinking Some Whisky after it. After we had Done Mr. Teeling called me over to him and Dr. Dickson who were Sitting beside each other and after [enquiring?] in the most affectionate manner what acc[ts.] I had from my friends, Mr. Teeling took me by the hand, and in the most Soothing manner adressed me nearly in the following words. 'My Dear Bryson, you are a Young Man whome I am happy in being acquainted with, as you have always behaved yourself as became a Man and a United Irishman. You have bore with fortitude not only your own Sufferings but the wrong of your much loved friends. Hitherto you have always been in hopes of being one Day or other released, but I am Sorry to tell you that in that Uncle whome you once thought your friend you have your bitterest enemy, and one who will never rest till he has you Sent out of the country; and I am Sorry to Say that I fear he is to[o] near having his Designs acomplished.[7] Twould be useless for me to recomend to you any line of conduct as I do not at present know what your Situation may be and I make no Doubt but you will always Support the character that you have Suffered So much for. I shall only say that in whatever Situation of Life you are placed, be assured that according as you behave so you will be treated. Prepare then, my Dear friend, for your removal which I much fear will take place tomorrow morning and always Recolect the Duty you owe to your God, your Country and your friends and that you may finaly triumph over your enemys is the Sincere wish of your friend.'

After he had finished I made what enquiry I could and found that had we had fair weather we would have Gone to Town that night. Of course we had to expect them early in the morning, for which we prepared, and about 9 in the Morning[8] we were called on and after bidding our friends a Last Adieu we proceeded to Belfast where we were kindly received by Mrs. Dickson and Miss —— who had been waiting for us to hear what news from the Ship. Immediately on Going into the

Prov[ost Prison] I Sat down to write to my Mother but found it impossible and Mr. Stavely[9] came in and told me he would write the next morning if I would leave him her adress, which I accordingly did and at the Same time told him my Situation and begged of him to accomodate me with a Guinea. He told me he was Sorry that he had it not in his power to Do it, as he had not So much money in his possession, and turning about he bid me Good Morning. He was not Long Left the room till Priests Fitzsumons[10] and McGinnis[11] came in. I was introduced by the Latter to the former and after mutual enquirys about common place things Priest Fitzsumons called me aside and told me that, understanding that I was Going off without any previous notice, he had called on me to offer his Services as in all prob[ab]ility, Said he, you are but ill provided for the journey. In Saying which he put into my hand a five Guinea note which he begged me to except [*accept*]. Had the Sum been less I would have taken it without any hesitation, but as I could not See any probable method by which he could be paid I would not take it, although he Seemed a Great deal hurt at my refusal. Upon their Leaving me I walked down Stairs and by chance met with Mrs. Tilly. Her I asked to Go to Mr. Colvin[12] and ask him for either half a Guinea or a whole one. In a few minutes She returned with Mr. Colvin's Complements to Mr. Bryson and he was Sorry that it was not in his power to Serve him. I would now have been Glad that I had excepted Mr. Fitzsumon's offer, but as we were now on the Street Surrounded by about 50 of the Lankishire Light Dragoons I had nothing Left me but to Depend on providence for my Subsistence.

On Leaving Belfast I was three Shillings in Debt to Mr. Dickey and had just half that Sum in my pocket. We arrived in Lisburn about 4 in the Evening and after Standing about half an hour in the Street we were conducted to the Guard House where we had the pleasure of beholding a Good fire, but as we were but Strangers we could not expect any more of it without paying for it and as this did not well answer me I contented myself with Looking at it and Sat down at the other end of the room. We were but a few minutes in untill Mrs. Munro[13] came and asked to See us, but as Soon as the officer understood who She was he ordered her about her business, after which I Laid Down on the boards and began to turn the past transactions that I had been engaged in in my mind, what the probable consequence of our present journey would be and what the Situation of my friends might be. At that moment I was roused from this by one of the men telling me that he was affraid that Mr. Dickey's pocket would be picked, as he was lying down between two soldiers and both his Pockets were open. Upon this I rose and went and waked Mr. Dickey, but it was too Late as he had Lost five Guineas and a half; and as my Sole Dependence had been placed on him I was now worse off than Ever and I now began Seriously to think on what means I Should fall upon in order to Get money to carry me I know not where.

At length I resolved to write to Colonel Lumley,[14] who at that time had the Command of the Town; and as Soon as I had my letter finished I Shewed it to Some of the rest and they agreed that it Should be Signed by them all. As Soon as this was done we Sent it off and I waited with the Greatest impatience for an answer, but as we had none at 12 OClock I began and wrote [another?] and Gave it to One of the Men that I was acquainted with, who Said he would put it in the Post Office in the Morning. About two OClock the Colonel made his appearance and after Blackguarding us a while he told us he had Received a Letter from us and that he would think of it and Let us know before we went away whether he would pay us or not, but he believed the Greatest Service he could do his Majesty would be to Let us Die by the road, for, Said he, there will be a pretty acc$^{t.}$ of you if ever they make Soldiers of you. Upon this he went away and in a Quarter of an hour he came back and paid us a Shilling for that day's march and told us that we would for the time to come be paid by whatever Officer had charge of us.

We were called out about an hour before Day Light and after waiting Some time we were marched off. The snow was about ten inches Deep and was falling very fast at that time. When it began to Get a little Clear I perceived the Officer to be an Old Acquaintance of mine and as Soon as he perceived me he asked me, with an oath, what brought me there. Your Colonel, I answered. He Said he was certain that the Colonel did not wish to have me Sent away, as he had often heard him Say that he expected that my friends would be able to persuade me to Go into his own Reg^t. But, Said he, your Bundle Seems to be heavy, you had better Give it to one of the men and he will carry it for you. This you may be Sure I very redily complied with. In a little time I asked him to Set a Stop at the first house to Get a Drink. [We marched to?] a House at Some distance and when we came up he had brought out the people's churn about half full of milk and a large jug, out of which he made us all Drink and then carried it in again. When we came in Sight of Hilsborough he asked us if we wished to Stop and as we had not wished to Stop here[15] he proceeded on to Dromore, where we were put into an old market house, one half of which was water proof and the other not. The latter of these fell to our Lott as there was a Corps of Yeomen that were Going to parade [which] had taken possession of the other. These were to be our Guard and when one of our men asked for Liberty to Send out for Some bread and cheese, one of the Yeomen very politely offered to Go for it. But instead of bringing that he brought a bottle of whiskey and treated his Comrades with it. Nor would he Give the poor fellow a Single Drop of it. When the officer came in I went forward and told him and had the Satisfaction of Seeing him put in the Stocks; and [he] had to pay the money back.

From Dromore we proceeded to Banbridge where we Stopped about half an hour upon the Street opposite an Inn and the most of the men took Some refreshment. For my part, I would take none and as all the others were Drinking I was rather Singular, which an old lady in an adjoining window espying came out and enquired if I was unwell. I told her I was not. She Said She was Glad of it for, Said She, I fancied that it was on that acc^t. you refused to Drink with your companions. But, added She, you must not refuse to Drink with me. Saying which, She called her daughter and told her to bring her a bottle of wine, which as Soon as She had received She gave me, Saying: 'you are better acquainted with your Companions than me and you will Oblidge me by Giving any of them that you think Deserving of it a Glass and if that is not Sufficient, I will bring you more; and it would Give me a Great Deal of pleasure to be able to assist you in any other thing.' By the time that the One was Drank, the officer made his appearance and asked in a very Surley tone what She was doing there. 'A common act of Civility,' Said She, 'and I am Sure you are too much of a Gentleman to prevent me.' He bowed and in a few minutes ordered the Guard to proceed. Upon which She wished us a pleasant journey and Seemingly with a heavy heart went into her house.

From this we made no Stop till we came to a place called the halfway house and, If I recolect right, we were then about 8 miles from Newry. It was now Dark and the road very Slippery. Of course we could not travel very fast and the night being intensly cold did not add much to our comfort. About ten OClock we reached Newry and were put into the Market house under the Care of a party of Hi[gh]landers. The officer that escorted us happened to be acquainted with the officer on Duty and as we had Suffered So much the preceeding night by being along with the Guard, he very kindly Spoke to the Hi[gh]land man and he abandoned his Guard Room to Six of us that the other recommended. Of course we had a Good fire to ourselves, which by that time was the Greatest blessing that we could Look for.

About ten minutes after we went in we were told that a Gentleman and Lady enquired for Dickey and Bryson. We went out and the Lady enquired if we knew Miss —— of Belfast. We answered in the affirmative. She was happy to See us Since it was our fate to pass that way. 'Go, John,' Said She to the young man, 'and tell my Mother that they are arrived and I will wait till you return.' While the young man was gone She told us that She had that Day received a Letter from her friend Miss —— in Belfast, Letting her know that we were to pass through Newry and begged her to pay every attention in her powers to me. 'My father is not at home,' Said She, 'as he would have come to See you himself, but I expect him every moment.' Just as She finished her father made his appearance attended by two men, one carrying a tea board and the other a Bed. As Soon as we had finished our Supper he told us we must excuse him for he could neither Stop there nor would it be possible for him to See us in the Morning, as he was Oblidged to Go to See a patient a considerable distance from town and he did not know when he would return. 'But', Said he, 'Maria will call and See you in the morning.'

He had not been long Gone when two other Gentlemen came and asked for us. One of these was the Gentleman who gave me the Money. The other would not tell us his name, although Mr. Dickey and I were with him and others the Greater part of the next day, which we Spent as agreeably as people in our Situation could be Supposed to Do. As we neither wanted Company nor wine Miss H —— came to See us in the Evening and made tea for us; and about 9 bid us an affectionate Adieu and the next morning by 8 OClock we left Newry and proceeded on our rout[e] to Dundalk.

The first part of this Days march was one continued Scene of disappointment, as we only climbed one Hill to See one Still higher, nor was it till we got halfway that we began to descend. The tops of these Mountains are by far the worst land I ever Saw. Indeed, they produce almost nothing but Turf, Stones and little poneys that you could with ease cary in your arms. When we came within Sight of Jones Town[16] we began to think that these dreary prospects were at an end, but we were only coming to the Worst. From ascending the next hill we found that instead of Getting better, it grew worse. The hills now were covered with large rolling Stones and not the least appearance of Soil of any kind. 'The Worst part of our Mountain', Said I, 'is a garden when compared to this.'

We were now at the foot of a Small hill which when we ascended I was Struck with Electrick force at beholding the Scene that presented itself to my View. The road ran directly through the Bottom of a valley called Ravens Dell[17] and on the one Side you beheld the Side of the Mountain Covered with Stones which Seemed to threaten inst[ant] Destruction and the other Covered with trees interspersed with Cottages and Summer houses. At the bottom, on this Side [of] the road, there is a River on which the Gentleman who Lives on the place has errected Machinery for bleaching Linen. His house, though not very

Superb, is nevertheless handsome and adds much to the Beauty of the place.

About five in the Evening we entered Dundalk and were all put into one room in the jail without Even a Seat to Sit on. In this Situation we remained about an hour, at the end of which time the jailer[18] called us into the hall where he paired us as unequal as possible and then took us to Different Cells. For my part I was paired with an Orange Man and the room we went into was full of Men all Stripped who had been fighting. The jailer, however, Soon made peace, but it did not Last Long, for the moment he turned his back they began to it as fresh as ever. For my part it gave me no concern while they Let me alone, but when one of them appealed to me and then asked me to become his Second, I then began to feel rather uneasy. However I resolved not to interfere, be the consequence what it might, which So exasper[at]ed the fellow that he Swore he would beat me if I did not help him to beat the other. My companion the Orangeman had by this time told them who he was and who I was, upon which they were all agreed in a twinkling; now they all Successively bantered me to fight them.

Swearing they would make me a Croppy[19] in Earnest, I was just beginning to Loose all patience (the consequence of which would probably have been fatal to me) when the jailer made his appearance, attended by a Gentleman Dressed in black, which Soon put an end to their hopes of hurting the Croppy. The jailer on his entrance asked me if my name was Bryson. I told him it was; he asked me if I was related to the Revd. And[w.] Bryson of that place and upon my answering in the affirmative he shook me very kindly by the hand and Said he was very Sorry to See me in Such a place.[20] The other did the same and added: 'as Soon as I heard that your name was Bryson I came down to see you; and you will Oblidge me much by excepting [*accepting*] part of my bed.' 'Are you an inmate of this place,' Said I? 'Yes, by Jesus, that he is,' Said the jailer, 'and as honest a man as is in the County of Louth.' I thanked the jailer for this piece of information and we proceeded to the Gentleman's room, where we had a Very Good Supper and Some punch. He proved to be a Mr. O'Hare, who had been in prison near twelve

Months and his tryal cost him near £100. He would have Sent out for Mrs. Bryson had I permitted him, but as we were all together Unacquainted with each other I thought it better not.

Mr. O'Hare had our breakfast ready by five in the morning and as Soon as we had Done we began our March to Drogheda. I had almost forgot to tell you that the officer [previously in charge?] of us took a french leave of us without paying us our Subsistence. The officer that had charge of us from Dundalk to Drogheda would not allow us to Stop for any refreshment untill we came within Sight of the Latter and then we could not Get anything to eat as the woman who kept the house Declared that She had only one Small piece of Bread, which She offered us. The officer treated us to a pint of Beer each and then we proceeded into town.

On our arrival we were Shut into the Court House where we remained about two hours and then were conducted to the jail. We found the jailer a fine Gentleman and a Yeoman.[21] The first thing he did was to pair us and luckily for us both Dickey and me were put together. We were put into one of the Low Cells and on my Steping in I found myself up to my knees in water. Dickey refused to enter without Light, but it was to no purpose for he [the jailer] Soon found a way to make him enter. He called one of his Turnkeys, who with a Box on the ear made him enter on all fours. By his fall he made a Considerable noise in the water, upon which a Voice issued from the corner calling 'who comes there?' I answered, 'a friend'. 'If you are a friend,' Said the Voice, 'you had Better keep a little more to the right, as the floor is not so wet there.' By this time Dickey had Got himself Gathered up and we took the Person's advice and by the time that we Got to the foot of his Bed we found the place, though not Dry, yet considerably Better than it was at the Door.

We presently began to ask the Person in the Corner Some Questions about the Situation of the place and whether it would not be preferable to Get a Light for a little time. He told us that Mother Murphy would be at the pump in a Little time and that if we would Speak to her, She would probably Get us a Candle. Upon this I took my Stand at the window and in ab[ou]t half an Hour She made her appearance. As Soon as I heard her at the place I called her and told her how we were Situated. 'Well Joy,' Said She, 'what Do you wish me to do for you?' 'We wish to Get Something to Eat, Drink and a Candle to Let us See to make a Bed,' Said I, putting a Crown in her hand, which happened to be the Smallest change we had. On the receipt of this the Old Woman tripped away as Light as a feather and in a little time appeared with a Candle, a three penny loaf, Some Cheese and a pint of whiskey. As Soon as She had handed the things into the window She Walked away and we Got nothing more for our five Shillings.

In return for Some of our Supper, our Companion Treated us with a little Straw on which we Sat Down and Drank one half of our Whiskey and eat half our Store of Bread and Cheese. The remainder we reserved for Breakfast, which we laid up carefully in an old Window and again sat down on our Straw, where we Sat and Sometimes Slept and Sometimes Chatted till we Saw Daylight begin to appear. Upon which we Got up to prepare for Marching, But upon Visiting the old window we found all our Bread and Cheese carried away by the Rats, in Doing which they had upset the Bottle and Spiled the Whiskey, So that we were now as badly Situated as ever. At that time of the morning, however, it was impossible to Get any thing, So we were Oblidged to Start without Breaking our fast.

We were this Day escorted by a party of heavy Dragoons, the officer of which would not allow us to Stop for to Get a Drink of water untill we came to the Man of War tavern. Here we Stopped at a Barrack in order to Get a fresh escort. But the commanding officer would neither take charge of us nor allow his men to Do it, in consequence of which the former one had to proceed. While we Stopped here the Guard would not allow us to Send for either Bread or water, so we proceeded to Swords in hopes of Getting Some there. In this we were again Disapointed, as we were not allowed to Stop. Dickey and I were fortunate enough to persuade a woman to Send a Boy after us with Some Bread and Beer, the latter of which we Got But our Lieut. Said that he was full as hungry as us and he would keep the Bread.

Just as the Clock Struck ten we entered Dublin and in about half an hour we found ourselves at the Gate of the Provost Prison. The Marshal was Gone to Bed, So we had to Stand in the Yard till his highness Got up. When he made his appearance he put the one half of us with him and, without any light to let us See where to Go, he put us all into a large room which was So full already that we found it impossible to Get room either to Sit or Lye down. We Stood in this place ab[ou]t half an hour and then the Jailer made his appearance with a light. We complained Bitterly that we could not Get Lying Down [space] after our March, But he Soon told us that we were But Strangers and that we must pay for any acco-modation of that Sort that we wished for. We told him that if he would put us into any place where we could Lye Down, we would pay him whatever he would Charge us in the morning. He Said he would try if he could Do anything for us. After Some time he returned and took Six of us along with him into the Black hole, where were 2 Barrack Bed-steads over which was thrown an old Sail. On these we were prepared to Lye Down, not expecting to get anything for Supper. The jailer, how-ever, asked us if we Did not want anything to eat, Saying that he wished to Do everything he could for any prisoner that came from the north, on acc[t.] of our country Man Mr. Teeling[22] who, added he, Staid in this place and Slept on that Bed all the time that he was here.

We axcepted his offer of Getting Some Bread and Cheese for Sup-per and after that went to Bed. What he Said, however, of Mr. T. pre-vented me from Sleeping for Some Time and after all the rest were Sleeping I thought I heard Some person Slip into the room. The Gloomy Ideas that had just been passing in my mind made me for a moment feel a little frighted, but a Minute's Examination made me think that It was wholly occasioned by the Reflections that I had been making. I listened, however, to See if I could hear any more noise, but as [it] was Silent as the Grave I now turned my Self in the Bed, intend-ing to Go to Sleep. Upon [which] a Shrill Voice Bawled out, 'Mother of Jesus Defend me. Who are you, in the name of St. Patrick?' The manner of the exclamation and the Language and Vain that it was uttered in made me, in Spite of the remaining part of my fears, Burst

out into a Loud fit of Laughter, which So incensed the Connaught man
that he Began to Blaze about him with his Shillila,[23] which he took care
to have in his hand. As Soon as I could I asked him who he was that
came there to Disturb People at that time of Night. 'By Saint Patrick,'
Said he, 'you vagabond, I will let you know who I am.' So Saying, he
struck at where he heard my Voice proceed from, but fortunately for
my Pericranium he was So near me that the Stick Struck ag[ains]t the
Wall. By this time the other Men were all awakened and we resolved
to Get up and Lay hold of the Madman, for Such we judged him to Be.
When he found that there were So many of us, he began to call out for
mercy and in token of his Peaceful Disposition he threw away his
Shililla. Our only fear now was that if we went to Bed again that he
would open Some of our Bundles and Rob us of our Cloathes. He now
told us his name was Pat, that he was a Prisoner and that he had been
Serv[an]t to the Late Mr. Teeling. We began from then to harbour a Better opinion of our Companion and in a little time we all went to Bed
and I do not Recolect ever Sleeping Sounder than I did that Night. In
the Morning, however, I found myself So Stiff that it was with considerable Difficulty I could put on my cloathes. Although the Morning was
pretty far advanced, we had not the least glimer of Light. Of course, we
had Some Difficulty in finding our Bundles. In looking for mine I happened to Stumble on our Companion who had given us So much trouble over night, upon which he roared aloud. This was the first thing that
Brought him to our recolection and we now began to make very merry
about the fear that all parties had been in.

This helped to pass the time till the Keeper came to open our Door.
We now Sallied forth into the Yard and the Morning Being very cold I
began to walk to and fro in order to warm myself. I had made but a few
turns till a french officer came out and began to the Same exercise and
in the course we met ocationaly and both would leave the clear path.
As I had not the Least Idea that I could make myself understood, I had
not thought of Speaking to him. At length, however, he acosted me in
pretty Good English and after enquiring where I was from he asked me
If I would walk up Stairs and Drink a Glass of Whisky with him. After

which, Said he, we will renew our walk. To this I consented and as Soon as we came down he began to enquire minutely about the Situation of the North of Ireland. Having Satisfied him as far as possible in regard to the State of the Country, he began to enquire about my own particular Situation and prospects. In Satisfying him on this head, I had necessarily to mention Belfast, upon which he asked me if I was acquainted with any of the Late Mr. Teeling's friends in that Neighbourhood. On my telling him that I had So Lately parted [from] his father, he took my hand and Drew me after him to his room and introduced me to the rest of his Companions, from all of whom I received the fraternal Embrace and then Sat down to breakfast, after which, taking me by the hand, he proposed walking. 'As a United Irishman,' Said he, 'I pitied and respected you at first Light, but as the friend and acquaintance of Mr. Teeling I love you as my Brother.' I now told him that I would introduce him to Some more of my Countrymen who were Good Republicans, upon which we went into the Black hole where they were at Breakfast on Bread and Beer. He told them he Supposed they would think it hard fare but, Said he, 'the Soldier Desire no better.'

When the Hour of Muster came he left us, after which we agreed that as there was a probability of our Staying Some time in there, We would endeavour to Bribe the Keeper to have us put into the Marshalsea.[24] With this intention, as Soon as muster was over we waited on him and after returning him thanks for his kindness to us the Preceding night, we handed him a Guinea, telling him that we would pay him for any accomodation of that Sort that he would Give us. Our Keeper had the money on the top of his finger and looked Sometimes at it and Sometimes at us. At length, on Swearing a Great Oath he Said he would just Begin with us as he meant to end, upon which he returned us fifteen Shillings, telling us that he would only Charge us One Shilling Each for the priviledge of Sleeping in a Separate apartment, and he was Sure it was as cheap at that as Bulls Beef was at one peny per pound. Saying which, he bid us Good morning.

We now began to Consult on what we Should Do next. Some were for Staying on in that place, But as this did not by any means Suit the preasant State of my finances, I avowed my Determination of abandoning it, which Determination was at Length Carried Nem. Con. Nothing now remained but to make it known to the Keeper and this every one threw on his Neighbour. At length, I offered to be the one if Dickey would acompany me, which he agreed to. We waited on him, But Excommunication was a Prayer Compared to what we Got from him. Luckily, however, he Durst not Strike as Long as we behaved ourselves with Proper Submission, and this was all we cared for. While we were Gone the rest Gathered up all our things, so that when the Enraged Keeper came to turn us out and lock the Door, he found nothing But an Empty Bottle to wreak his Vengeance on, which he did by Dashing it to Pieces.

As Soon as the Commisary Came down I told him how the Keeper had treated us. 'Ay,' Said he, 'and that is not the Worst of it, for he has just Given Orders that you are not to Get any thing out of his house and he will neither Give you Blankets nor Straw to lye on tonight, and Because he heard of your Being in our room this morning, he refused to let me have a Gallon of Whiskey just now. But as Soon as Major Blunt comes, I will See who is Master here, him or the Keeper. In the meantime', Said he, 'you and your companions must Eat Dinner with me, as I am convinced that you will not be able to Get any any other where.'

This you may be Sure was accepted of and by the time we had Done it was Dark and the Keeper was Calling for us to be locked up for the Night. On Going away the Commissary oblidged us to axcept of two pair of Blankets and on Opening them in order to make our Beds we found a Quantity of Bread & Cheese and 3 Bottles of Whisky, accompanied by a note telling us that it would be all Little enough to pay our footing. Before we found this, we had been asked more than once for this, but as it was impossible to Get any thing at that time of night we had prevailed on them to allow us to Stay that night, for which we were to pay them Double in the morning.

You will perhaps be Surprised that prisoners Should treat one another in this Manner. But it is an established maxim that no prisoner Shall be allowed to Sleep in any room untill he has paid whatever a

Majority of the Prisoners in that room think proper, in order to free him of the place, and you need not wonder at the hard Conditions that they exacted of us when you are told that the Greater part of the Prisoners in the room that we were now put in were Deserters.

As Soon as our Whisky was out we went to Bed, but not to Sleep. This no person could expect to find in this place. The room we were in was about 16 feet Square, in which there were cramed 120 prisoners, none of which had any thing But Straw to Lye on, and this they Shaked every night and Burned all the Dirt, the heat and smoak of which, added to the noise of the Drunken and profane, certainly rendered [this room] as compleat an emblem of the place of torment as any that is to be found on earth.

Never did poor Wretch want with more anxiety than I did for to See Day Light. On the first appearance of which I Got up and Began to Dress myself and Before I had finished we were all called by Name and Paraded in the Yard. From this we went to the Keeper's room and after Being paired as equally as Possible we were handcuffed two & two and then Brought back into the Yard again. After Standing about half an hour we began to walk about, which the Keeper perceiving very humanely Called us all together and with a Rope tied us all together and then tied the two ends to Stapels in the wall. In this State we remained till 12 OClock, and after Bidding Good by to our Good Comisary, we were Marched off by two Companies of Foot. It appeared that we were the first that had been Served in this Manner, as we were followed by Hundreds of Men, Women and Children untill we were as far out of the City as Kilmainham, where the Party halted and Dispersed them. From this place the roads were So bad that we could Scarce proceed and by the time we reached —— ,[25] which is only five miles from Dublin, it was almost night.

Notwithstanding this, we were to have proceeded as far as Naas, but fortunately for us the officer that was to have taken us in Charge was indisposed. Of course, we had to remain till Morning in the Guard House, which we found inhabited by the Waterford Militia, from whom we experienced the Kindest treatment of any we had yet rec[eive]d. The Sergeant Did every thing in his power for us, except taking our handcuffs off, and this was a favour we did not now expect till we would arrive at our Destined Part. The Soldiers Gave every one that they found to be United Irishmen Beds and the others they would not allow to lye by the fire.

In the morning We Got Breakfast and at Nine in the Morning we began our journey in the fresh. In the course of this Day's march we had more acts of Cruelty told us of the Rebels that haunted the Mountains on our Left[26] than Bounapart would perform in three Campaigns with 100 thousand Frenchmen at his heels. About half past 2 OClock we entered Naas, which we found fortified by Large Ditches, three across each Street, in the Center whereof was a Gate wide enough to admit the Mail and on each Side a 10 pounder Mounted with the matches Burning. We were marched first to the Guard house and from there to the jail yard. As they Did not untie us on putting us into the Yard, we thought that we could not Do less than caste our Bands [*i.e. ropes*], which we did, and then began to walk about. But the Yard being very Dirty, the handcuffs incomoded us Very much, as one of us had always to walk in the mud. It presently occured to me that a Knife of Gawin Watts[27] that I had Brought away with me, in which was a Butter hook, would answer every purpose of a key and in trying the Experiment had the Satisfaction to find that it opened them as fast as the Keys Did. Of course we Soon disengaged our Selves of this incumbrance, which done we walked at our ease till after 5 OClock, when we were put into the jail.

Dickey, Adams[28] and me were turned into a Long Gallery and told to Shift for ourselves as well as we could. We found Several Doors, but all [were] Locked and the place was So Dark that we were oblidged to tread with caution, Least we Should Break our Legs over a parcel of turf that were Scattered about. After trying in Vain for a Considerable time we agreed to Sit Down and wait the event with patience. We naturally began to talk about the stories that had been told us about the Rebels, the Greater part of which we aproved. This led us to talk over the old affairs at home. Before we had Discussed long on this Subject, a Voice called out: 'Dam the Rebels' and was quickly answered by another: 'Dam the Orangemen'. This made us begin to Look about us pretty Sharply and at Length we perceived that we had been Listened [to] by Some persons on the outside of the Gate. But as Soon as they found themselves Discovered, they Dispersed. As the other Voice Seemed to come from Some person further on in our Gallery, we resolved to attempt to find them. On reaching the end of the passage, we found that it ran of[f] to the One Side and here were plenty of Prisoners Sitting round Good fires. We went into the Second as it did . . .[29]

Seeing that the first room was full, we pushed forward to the Second, in which we found three men also Seated round a Good fire. None of them, however, for Some time offered to rise or Bid us come near the fire, which Did not Give us a very favourable opinion of them. After Sitting Behind backs for Some time, I at length Got up and advised one of them to change Seats with me. The Fellow, by the by, had not a very promising countenance. I did not expect, however, that he would [have] refused me. After thinking with himself for a few moments, he answered in a very Loud murmer: 'By J——s, Boy, I would not rise from this fire for the Best Orangeman in Ireland and if you intend to Sit Down by this fire, you must tell us where you come from, where you are going, and who you are, 'for', Says he, 'the Devel a Bit of me naes any thing about you, at all at all. But mind Ye, By St. Patrick, if you are an Orange Man' (and he seized the Tongs) 'Should I be Shot as my Brothers were, I will take Some of your Liver Before Morning.'

As I had neither time nor inclination to Satisfy him, I was oblidged to resume my Seat, Behind Backs again, and had not the Jailer[30] come in we Should have Sat there till morning. As Soon as he made his appearance, they all Got up and the one that had Spake So natty to me asked him in the Same tone that he Spake to me in, if he had no other Cell to put Orangemen in than that [one], adding: 'you Seem to wish to have me hanged for murder, as you would not always cram them in here.' The jailer's answer was in Irish, So I could not understand it. It produced an instantaneous change in Both the Looks and Behaviour of those to whome it was addressed, as they immediately invited us to Sit forward to the fire and Mr. O'Sullivan went out with the Jailer. As what the Jailer had Said to them had put them into Good humour and the Goodness of the fire in a Little time producing the Same effects on us, we Soon began to Strike up a little conversation with each other and Before O'Sullivan returned we had his whole history from one of his comrades.

His Father was one of the most respectful [*respectable*] farmers within 20 miles of where he lived and had 4 Sons and 2 daughters. At the commencement of the rebellion, the 3 Elder of the Sons had been very active and, of course, there was Soon a Large reward offered for their apprehension, to obtain which a number of Soldiers and Yeomen went in Search of them to their father's house. Not finding them, they took their father, Brother and Sisters and Said they would keep them untill they would find the others. Before they had proceeded far, however, the 3 Brothers, hearing how they were proceeding, followed and with Some others attempted to rescue them. With this intent They followed them Several miles, wishing to Let them proceed to a Certain Spot before they attacked them. On coming to the top of a hill, however, they found the Party had halted in the Valy and upon Looking at them for a little time, they Saw their Brother and father Bound to a tree and presently heard their Sisters call. Laying aside all fear for themselves, they rushed down the Hill and arrived just in time to Save the honour of their Sisters, [but] at the expense of their own lives. They both fell and along with them their Father. The Sisters made their escape and the infernal Plunderers, after cutting off the heads of the Deceased, carried them and their prisoners to Town in triumph, where they were immediately Paid the offered reward.

The man who Gave us this intelligence was one of the Party who had been engaged in the rescue, but Being fortunate enough to escape, he had returned in the evening and Buried his Comrades, in Doing which he had been taken on Suspicion and neither him nor the unfortunate O'Sullivan knew what fate awaited them.

When O'S. returned he had a large jug of Tea, Some Bread and Butter & a Bottle of whiskey which, he Said, the Jailer had Bestowed [on] him in order to make up friends with his Northern Brethren. We did not Stir while the Whiskey Lasted and during that time we Gave and rec[eive]d as General an acc^t. as we could of the State of the Country, the Depredations that had been committed on Both Sides etc. I found O'S. to be a young man of Good information and Liberal turn of mind.

Ab[ou]t 1 OClock the Jailer came to tell us we must put out our Lights, as the General had remarked [on] them and ordered him to handcuff us. Our friends now made their Beds and insisted that we Should Lye on them and they would Sit By the fire, as they could Sleep tomorrow when we would have to march through mud to the knees. This we refused, upon which they Swore that if we Sat by the fire, So would they, as they were determined not to Sleep on Beds and Let us Lye on the Ground. Finaly, we took the Beds and with Good Beds under us & plenty of Whiskey in us, we had a Good Sleep and the first thing we Saw when we awakened was plenty of tea and Eggs for our Breakfast, which we had Scarce time to Swallow till we were called upon and after thanking them for their Kindness we hurried off on our road to Kilcullen Bridge, the distance I do not now recolect.

It was ab[ou]t three OClock when we entered the town, Before which, on the top of a hill, is Errected a Large Battery which commands not only the town but a Large track [*tract*] of country about. At this time it was Garrisoned by the County Dublin Militia, who treated us very well, and the officer of the Guard allowed Dickey and I to Sit in his own Guard room, where we wrote a letter. Before we had finished which, the General came in and abused the officer very much for allowing us to write at all and on Going off, charged him on his Peril not to allow them to Go away till he would read them. This he promised, but by being Blind [he] was unable to execute [it], as neither of us wrote the most Supple hand.

Although the Officer was So kind as [to] allow us to write, he would not by any means allow our Handcuffs to be taken off, as he Said that it was very probable that the General would visit the Guard house in the course of the Night. Nor was he mistaken, for Ab[ou]t 2 in the morning he made his appearance, Dressed in his Morning Gown. But on finding that we were all handcuffed, he Said nothing.

Ab[ou]t 8 in the morning the officer and a Comp[an]y of the Militia made their appearance and we Set off once more. The officer might be ab[ou]t 13 year old and from his appearance a handkerchief to have applyd to his Nose would have answered him much Better than a Sword.[31] Before we had proceeded far we met a party from Carlow escorting 2 prisoners who were on their way from Geneva[32] to Dublin, their friends having obtained a Habeas Corpus for them.[33] While the officer Stopped to Speak to the Serg^t· we Learned from them that all our friends in Geneva were well and had been expecting us for Some time.

When we were about a mile Distant from the Royal Oak our officer asked us if we intended to Breakfast there. We told him we would, So on entering the Town he went to the Inn and Sent a few of us to every Publick house. The house that we went to could neither give us one thing nor another, in consequence of which we Sent a Deputation off to the officer to Beg of him to change our Quarters. As he had Breakfasted himself, he allowed us to Go to the Inn, But told us that if we called for our Breakfast, it would cost us 4 Shillings. 'And when you have done, you will be no better than when you Sat down, for by G——,' Said he, 'a Sucking Child would Eat all they Gave me.' In consequence of this Piece of information we called for Some Beer and he allowed one of the Men to Go and Buy us Some Bread & Cheese, on which he breakfasted as heartily as any of us.

On Sitting Down he ordered our hands to Be loosed, in Doing which he observed that my Rist was much hurt, upon which he asked me why I did not Get a[n] under Belt. I told him that it was the widest in Dublin. 'Well but', Said he, 'there are plenty of Smiths Between Dublin and the Royal Oak and you Should have had it altered.' 'You had better allow me to have it Done now,' Said I. He had no objection what-ever, provided that I would pay the Expense, but 'by G——,' Said he, 'I have not so much money as will pay for my Dinner and that was the reason that I eat so heartily of your Bread & Cheese.' As Soon as the Smith appeared, they all began to complain of their hands being hurt. He would not allow any of them to be attended but mine, as none of their wrists appeared hurt. Before the Smith went away I Gave him 2

Glasses of Whiskey, which the officer observing Swore that I wanted to Bribe him. 'But Mr. Smith,' Said he, 'if you make it So wide that he can Get his hand out, I will find a way to pay you on my return.' He Said he would not and away he went. On his Return the Ring would easily hold both my hands. The Officer, however, was in to[o] Great a hurry to pay any attention to trifles, So we proceeded with it as it was.

Before we had traveled far my Companion Gave up and he [the officer] was Oblidged to press[34] a Car for him to Ride on and as the officer would not allow us to be loosed, I was oblidged to ride allong with him, which was the Severest trial I had met with yet, for the Day was intensly Cold and the road imensly rough. In consequence of which, I resolved that as Soon as I began to Get tired, I would pull my hand out of the Handcuff, Let the event be what it would. We had proceeded about 6 miles when the Road Got So rough that I could bear it no longer, So [I] Determined to Sit no longer. But by that time my hand was So much Swelled that I found it impossible to work it out. I therefore began to think whether I could open them with my knife, as formerly. Before I had Got my Knife opened, the officer perceived it and Gave one of his Corporals Strick [*strict*] charge to walk along Side of me all the way, as he Said that either I meant to Kill my Self or Some of the people that were on the car with me. I begged him to allow me to walk, as I was almost famished with the Cold, but he would not allow the handcuffs to be taken off. So I was oblidged to put up with my misfortune with the best Grace I could. Before we arrived at Carlow, however, I Got into Such a passion with Some of the people on the Car with me that my Blood Soon began to Circulate with its usual heat.

We arrived in Carlow about an hour before Sun Down and were in hopes of being taken Direct to the Jail, but the Jail of Carlow is either So much better or the Commanding Officer of the Town is So much more proud than any that we had yet met with, that we could not be allowed to aproach its hallowed walls till we had Done penance for half an hour at the foot of the Gallows, which is in front of a New Jail at present building there & on the Top of which were the heads of 3 of our Countrymen. The Barrack Stands at But a Small Distance from the Jail,

So we were Soon Surrounded by a Group of its motley Inhabitants. We found that they were part of the Downshire Militia, So we expected to find Some acquaintances among them. I was at Last asked by one of them how it was and what the Devil brought me there, and presently realised the person to be a Son of James Marre of N.T. [*Newtownards*], Commonly Called Scruffy Jamey. He did not, however, Give me time to answer him, but pointing to the heads (at which by this time a number of little Boys who were assembled were [hurling?] Stones) he asked me if I did not think they were very handsome, saying which he took up a Stone and threw it with Such force that, Striking one of the heads, it Dashed it in pieces. Upon which, the Rabble Gave 3 Cheers and he was the best fellow that could first Get hold of one of the pieces. Marre Got part of the face for his part and bringing it to me, he asked me again if it was not a Very handsom Countenance, at the Same time holding it up to my nose. I replied that I thought it a Very handsom one and that I thought that it resembled his Father Very much, for, Said I, 'there is not more Blood and Dirt on the upper lip of that Skeleton than there is Snuff and Snot on his'. This raised Such a laugh against him that he left us to our Selves and in a Little time we were ordered off to the jail.

Our little Officer, notwithstanding his treatment of us on the road, yet on Giving us to the Jailer recommended us to him in the warmest manner, but you will perhaps think that he did this merely to Gain our favour at the moment, that we might not ask him for our pay, which he took care to cary away with him. The jailer, on his going away, called 6 of us up into the Debtor's Rooms and Left us there with a Good fire to warm us, telling us that as Soon as he had Disposed of the rest he would return & take off our Handcuffs. He returned in about half an hour and took all their Handcuffs but mine. But Some thing had Gone wrong with the Lock and none of the keys would open it, & it being then to[o] late for any person to be admitted into the jail, he told us that we must content ourselves to let them remain on till Morning, when he would Get a Smith to pick the lock. I told him I would Save him the trouble, for I am Determined that off they Shall be, & that before many minutes. 'I See what you mean,' Said he, Saying which he took the pike in his hand

& walked Down Stairs. I was a little disapointed, but tooke out my knife, thinking that I would be able to open them with the same faculty that I did in Naas, but I was wretchedly disapointed, for the point being broke off the Staple of the lock, My knife would not catch on it, as my hand continued So much Swelled as to render it impossible to work it out.

I began to look about for Some thing with which I might break the lock. In this I had been the means of disapointing myself, as the pike was the only thing in the room wherewith I could have oppened it. At last, however, it occured to me that by fixing the lock on a bolt of our door I might be able to thrust it off. My companion, however, did not like to try the experiment, as his arm was even worse than mine. I insisted on it, however, & he at Length consented, but as we could not turn ourselves head over heels, we could not twist the lock. At length I Got So Angry that I resolved that I would either break the lock or my arm, and in the Situation I was in I would as Soon the Latter had been the case as the former. Happening to have a Good Strong cord in my pocket, I made Adams Lash the Lock to the Staple &, Setting my foot to the Bottom of the Door, I threw my Self back with Such force as to break the Lock all to pieces, and my head was near meeting the Same fate. I Got off, however, with Seeing the Greater part of the Skin off the back of my hand. My partner, who had no Idea of what I was Going to Do, Got Such a tug that he Swore he would as Soon have Got a Shock from an Electrick wheel.

As Soon as I was sensible of the Damage we had Sustained, I Gathered up the fragments of the handcuffs and threw them into the River Barrow, which runs by the end of the Jail. I was just Sat down comfortably by the fire when the Jailer came in with Some Bread & Beer for our Dinner. He asked me how I had got my handcuffs off. I told him they had been So Long coming with Dinner that I had eat them. So Saying, I caught up a piece of Bread and began to eat with as much Voraciousness as if I had not Seen [a] meal before for a week. I believe he realy thought that I was in earnest, for he immediately ordered his man to bring more Bread, upon which the rest Set up Such a Laugh as much confounded the poor Jailer. I now began to think that we were making

him a Very poor return for his kindness. I therefore apologised to him
for treating him So badly and told him that he had made us So comfortable & happy by his kindness that we did not know how to make
enough of ourselves, begging at the Same time that he would not be
offended with us for our pleasantry. This So far pleased him that he Sat
down & ordered his man, instead of the Bread to bring him a Jug of
punch, to treat his friends from the North with.

In the course of Drinking the punch I told him what I had Done with
my handcuffs. 'Well,' Said he, 'the Devil Go with them. But you may
thank God that you have met with a friend who is able to accomodate
you with a fresh pair, for were the officers to know that you threw them
away, you would have to pay a visit to the Barrack Yard Before Breakfast in the morning, where you [would] Get Something that you would
perhaps think as hard to Digest as the Handcuffs had you realy eat them.
But you must not be alarmed, for I have a pair that [I will] make at your
Service.' I thanked him for his kindness and he Left us to Go & Lock up
Some of the prisoners, telling us not to Go to Bed, for he would be in
to See me again in half an hour, in which he was as Good as his word,
for he returned bringing with him 2 beds & a Sufficient Quantum of
Blankets & after Giving us another jug of punch he bade us Good night
& we went to bed well pleased with our accomodations.

The next morning we were up by Day Light expecting to Set out for
Kilkenny, but owing to Some neglect we Did not Get out till twelve
OClock, when it was therefore too Late for to proceed, So were
remanded back. The Jailer did not Visit us all Day, So we began to think
that he had forgot us. But as Soon as it was Dark he made his appearance, telling us that he had done nothing all Day but call us all Rascals
& now, Said he, I am come to make you amends by treating you to your
Supper, which he did in his own Room, where we staid till ten OClock
& then turned in.

The next day we were up at an early hour, but we were almost as ill
Served as the preceding one, or rather, we were worse for we were
Detained upwards of three hours, kept Standing in the Street before we
began our March, which was not till Eleven OClock. On acc^t· of which,

They intended to Stop at Laughlin Bridge,[35] which was but 6 miles from Carlow. Well might the poet Sing 'the banks of the Sweet Barrow', for of all the Country I had yet Seen, this was the most Delightful, Though not So romantic as Evensdale, yet the High State of Cultivation that presented itself to View and the Numerous Lighters plying up & Down more than compensated for the want of that romantic appearance to which the Dale owes its Beauty.

We arrived in Laughlin Bridge about 1 OClock, but to our mortification we found no Military there but the yeoman who, Seeing 23 rough looking [blank], absolutely refused to take any thing to Do with us. In Vain the officer both entreated and then threatened him. He would neither hear Escort, nor be intimidated by fear. So we were under the necessity of proceed[ing] to Kilkenny, then distant 13 miles. The officer, to assist us as much as possible, took off our handcuffs & pressed 2 Cars to cary our baggage and assist the Lame. It was the close of the Evening before we arrived at Kilkenny, So were disapointed of Getting any [observation?] of the Town & particularly, of the Earl of Ormond's Stables, Said to be one of the handsomest buildings in Ireland.

We were marched directly to the Jail, which is a tolerable handsome Building but not very large, and at the time we arrived was So full that there was not a room for us to Go into. So we were Oblidged to take up our Residence in the Hall which passed through the middle of the jail from the Street into the Yard, and on which were three Huge Iron Gates, So that we had two of them between us and the Street and one between us and the Yard. The jailer received us Very Kindly and took off our handcuffs before he Left us (the officer had put them on before we came to the end of the Town). He told us he was Sorry he could not accomodate us better, but he thought that it would not be fair to turn any of his own family out to accomodate Strangers. 'But', Said he, 'any other thing that's in my power Shall be done for you. My wife will be here presently and She will Get you anything you want.' He had not been Gone [a] few minutes when a Very Respectable Woman and a Very handsome Daughter made their appearance at the Outer gate and from their being admitted without any Ceremony we concluded that they were the jailer's Wife & Daughter. 'Holy Prophet,' Said the former on Seeing us, 'who have we here?' 'Indeed & upon my own Shoul,' Said the Turnkey, 'I don't [k]now who they are, but I think that they are Decent looking men.' She came forward and asked where we were from and upon being Satisfied in that Respect, She called for the key & came in. She looked at us all from right to left. Without Saying a word [she] went to the Gate and Looked into the Yard for Some time. 'God help you,' She Said, 'You are all wet & Dirty & here is no fire to Dry you. Kitty,' Said she to her Daughter, 'I wish you would bring in Some coals in the chafery buck[et].' Kitty oblig'd and in a few moments we had a Good fire made, which Seemed to Give as much Satisfaction to the Mother & Daughter as it did Comfort to us.

She now began to ask us what we had Done, how long we had been prisoners, where we were Going, whether we were tried etc. etc., all of which we answered as well as we could. At length, all the rest Gathered about the fire but Dickey and I, of whom She began to enquire more particularly about the Rest of our fellow prisoners, of whome we Gave her the Best acc^t. we could. As Soon as she had learned all our [stories] She retired, Saying that She would be in in a few minutes again. We now began to make Some enquiries at Kitty about the State of the Country, whether there had been any United Irishmen hung there or not. She told us there had been a Great number & that there were three Heads upon the Gallows. Dickey asked her if She was not afraid to Live in the jail under Such circumstances. She replyd She was not, for that her father, Mother & herself had always did every thing in their power for the Sufferers & 'I believe that If the United Irishmen were to be in possession of the town in the morning that there is not a man in the County Kilkenny that would hurt us.'

Her mother returned in a few moments bringing a bottle of whiskey with her, which She Gave us and told us to Give none of it to any but Such as we knew. We Sett it round very Sparingly which, when she perceived, She told us that we might take what we pleased, as She was Determined not to take any of it Back. When each of us had taken a little of it, there was not more than the half of it made use of and we could not press it on her to take any of it back. So we laid it by till morning. This She also Objected to, but, Said She, 'I by no means wish you to Drink more than will Do you Good, but when I Give any thing of this Sort I wish as many as are worthy of it to be partakers; and were you not from a part of the Country for which I have the highest Respect, I would not treat you as I do. I am now Going to Shew you one of the [most] honest men that this Country has produced and although we are Oblidged to keep him Loaded with Irons, yet I hope you will not think the worse of either him or us on that acc^t.' Saying which, She took a key out of her pocket and put it in a Door that went into a Cell from that part of the Hall where we were. Before She opened the door, however, She told us to consider that when in the inside we would be in company with a Man in Women's cloathing, who was put there for a Spy, and turning to me: 'I think', Said She, 'you might be able to work him a little, but take care not to Let him have the Least Idea that you know any thing About him.'

She opened the Door & told the inhabitants that Some prisoners from the North had arrived & that She had no better place for them than the Hall, but I know that the prisoners in this Room will be as accomodating to them as possible, as they are Very much fatigued. As Soon as She had Done Speaking She went out & Kitty followed. There were Seven people in the Room, but none of them appeared very Singular except the one She mentioned as being Loaded with Irons. I had the wiskey in my hand & as Soon as we had Said how Do you, I asked him if he would take a little whiskey to keep up his Spirits. He Said he had no objections. Before I had filled the Glass, the Quondam Lady made her appearance & Introduced herself by asking me if I would accept a Seat at the fire. I Said I had no objections, provided She would first honour me So far as [to] Drink a Little whiskey with me. She Said She was always proud to be in company with people from the North. I helped her to a Glass & then Gave the bottle to Dickey & went to the fire with Madame, fully resolved that before her [*crossed out*] him & I parted, I would make him rue the Day that She [*crossed out*] he put on the petticoats to become a Spy. The Very appearance, however, of the [*illegible*] affected me So much that I felt it impossible to Speak to him with that freedom I wished, which, Dickey perceiving, Gave me a Little more whiskey which I Swallowed with the Very intention of making me mad.

As a Detail of what followed would neither be useful nor entertaining, I Shall pass over it, only Saying that in the course of an hour I had with the assistance of Some of the by Standers wrought him to Such a Degree that I was not Sure whether he would ever recover & for my part, I can only Say that I never was as much fatigued in my Life as when I Quitted that Room, which was not till the jailer and his wife came to Lock the Door at ten OClock. They were both So well pleased with what had happened [that] they made us (Dickey, Adams & I) go in and Sup with them, which partly paid me for the trouble I had in earning it.

After Supper, the jailer lamented that he could not accomodate us with a Bed, as he had all that he had hired out to the Debtors. The Mother Spoke a few words to the Daughter in Irish, who answered She would & presently they both went up Stairs. 'Don't you understand Irish?', Said the jailer. We answered, we did not. 'Then you do not know what was Said just now?' We answered, no. 'Well then,' Said he, 'my wife asked Kitty if She would not Spare one of her Beds for you & you heard her answer.' We objected to this, protesting that we would not deprive her of her bed. 'Fair & Softly,' Said he, 'you must Except [*accept*] that it is our province to command here & yours to obey' &, Said he, 'I am Sure that you want a bed as much as any person in the Town & If you please, we will Go and See whether they are Getting it ready or not.' When we went into our apartment we found them all asleep upon a parcel of clean Straw & in one corner the Ladies were making our Bed, which as Soon as they had finished they bid us Good night & we turned in to an excellent feather Bed & plenty of Blankets, from which we Did not rise till 8 oclock in the morning, when we were raised by an old woman who attended the jail with milk.

'Honeys,' Said the old woman, 'dont you want to buy any milk for your breakfast?' Each of us Got a pint, for which the old Lady only charged us a Halfpenny as we were Strangers. As we had been told over night that we would not Leave Kilkenny that Day, we made ourselves as comfortable as we could & the Jailer, at our request, allowed Some of the prisoners to Visit us, from whome we heard all the news of the country, but they were So Like what happened in your own that it is unnecessary to Report them. Neither the jailer, his wife, nor Kitty Spoke to us all day, but as Soon as it Grew Dark the former came & asked Dickey and I into his room. 'I want', Said he, 'to Serve you, if you think that none of the party will betray me. As It was dark when you came here, people could not redily See whether you were Handcuffed or not. Now your Guard is returned to Kilkenny, So if you thought that I might depend on the discretion of the Soldiers who are with you, I would retain all the Handcuffs, which would Serve us both, as they would be worth something to Sell.' We went & Spoke to them all & they Swore that If he would [keep the handcuffs], they would Suffer Death Rather than Say anything about the business. We then, agreeably to his directions, had them all to deny in the morning having any [handcuffs] with us.

The next morning, wen the Guard came & we were called out & our handcuffs asked for, the jailer replyd we had brought none with us. 'Well,' Said the Capt., 'I will have the pleasure of hang[ing] the first to Russle you. Jailer, bring me all the Handcuffs you have Got & I will pay you for them on my Return.' 'I have not Got a Single pair,' was the answer, 'nor do I believe you will be able to Get a pair in town.' 'Well, you must Get me Ropes, for I am determined not to move an inch till I have them Secured.' The jailer very reluctantly brought out a piece of Jack cord, with which he tyed a Couple who were in front & demanded more to do the remaining 4. 'I have not got an inch more,' Said our friend, 'nor do I think there is the Least ocation for taking any trouble with the Rest, as from the Recommendation Given of them by the Officer who brought them here, I would not be afraid to march them to Thomas Town my Self.' 'Well, I will take your word for once', So he Gave orders to proceed.

We had this Day the Strongest Guard we had yet been under, which consisted of a Company of the 29th Reg^t· & one of Heavy Dragoons. We began our march about 8 in the morning & had 20 miles to bring

us to Tho[ma]s Town. I believe the Distance is not So much, but they
were afraid to march us in the Direct road which Lay considerably
about and what was worse the roads were Very bad. I think I never Saw
a more fertile looking country, yet in all our march we Saw only one
Stack of Grain & that in the most miserable Situation, having neither
Thatch on it to defend it from the weather, nor Fence Round it to Keep
of[f] the cattle, of which there were Some hundreds about it. The
Country abounds with Lime Stone, of which they build their houses &
Ditches, which adds much to the beauty of the country. In one plough
which I saw Going, there were 4 Horses and 2 Oxen & they Seemed to
have more difficulty in this draught Than Hugh Stewart's two poneys
would be ploughing the Steepest part of his hill. Yet they were Good
Horses, but every furrow they made was as deep as a potatoe furrow in
most parts of your neighbourhood. They are oblidged to do this on acc[t.]
of the wetness of the Soil. They also make their Ridges Very narrow, So
that their fields, when in Grass, Resembles one of your potatoe ones. I
could not help thinking what curses Pottinger[36] would Give them, was
he to Start at here in one of them.

We arrived in Thomas Town a little before Dark. The town is Small
& Remarkable for nothing that I could See but a tolerable Good Stone
bridge over the River on which it Stands, part of which, however, has
been carried away by the Current & has not yet been reparred. We
found only 10 Soldiers in Town, all of whom were on Guard. The Rest
had Gone away to escort a party of prisoners that morning & Should
not Return till next evening. Our Capt. was at a loss what to do with
us, but at Last resolved to call in a party of the Yeoman Cavalry to aug-
ment the Guard & that he would proceed with us the next day to
Waterford.

The Guard House consisted of two rooms, in one of which there
was no fire, So we Resolved to take possession of it & Leave the Soldiers
of our party to Stay with their companions & the fire. The first yeoman
who made his appearance was the very picture of Thompson of
Comber, commonly called Satan, who immediately drew his Sword &
placed himself Sentry on our Door, which we immediately Shut. On

which, he came into the inside. Had my life been depending on the Issue, I could not [have] avoided laughing at the figure he cut, with his Sword in his hand & his face distorted with fear & his mouth as wide as my [shed?], Gulping as if he meant to devour every word that passed. 'Did you ever See the Devil upon two Sticks?', Said Stone to me. Before I had half done laughing at the Quixot like appearance of our hero, I replyd I had not. 'Well then,' Said he, 'I have the Honour to present to you Devil upon Two Legs', Saying which He took the afrighted Yeoman by the Shoulders & turned him round as you have Seen Some people twirl their Hat round the top of their Stick when they had nothing else to Say or do. Poor yeo[man] was bad enough before, but he now presented a figure truly Romantic. He Gaped till his face was as Long as my Arm, but we were laughing too loud for him to utter a word. At Length, half choaked with rage, he ran out of the room, Swearing he would find a way to make us Quit our fun. He went & Complained to the Sergeant, telling him how he had been treated. 'They Served you very well', Said he, 'if you were foolish enough to put up with it.' Still more enraged, he ran out Swearing he would make both him & us repent our folly. 'Stay,' Said the Serg$^{t.}$, 'I want to Speak to you before you Go. Hear [me], Laton, come back', and was by the Serg$^{t.}$ ordered disarmed & put in along with us as prisoner for leaving his post without being relieved.

We immediately began to tell each other how many Soldiers had been flogged for that crime when placed on common duty and from thence drew a conclusion what would be his fate who Left his post when on extraordinary duty. As we could not agree, we resolved to call a General Court Martial, but before we were able to carry our resolve into execution, the Capt. Came in, to whome he began to make his complaint on both the Serg$^{t.}$ & us. 'I am much surprised', Said the Capt., 'that these prisoners Should treat you badly, as they behaved with the Greatest propriety on the road. There must be Some misunderstanding in the business. Tell me, what did they do or Say to you?' 'Why, they called me the Devil on two Sticks, Laton Beezlebub & every bad name they could think of, and, for the Serg$^{t.}$, he would neither Give me any Satisfaction nor allow me to Go to you to complain on Him. And now, because I was Loyal enough to Volunteer my Self in his Majesty's Service, I am made a prisoner & put in along with a parcel of Cropys, who would take my Life if they durst. But I am resolved to Let the General know as Soon as I go to Waterford.' 'Are you?', Said the Capt., 'then you may Look to the General for your Satisfaction, and unless the Serg^t. thinks proper to release you, you may remain till the General does.' By this time 2 more of the yeomen were come, who interposed in behalf of their fellow Soldier & he was released. And the other 2 Saying that they would be responsible for us, he was dismissed, not a little mortified that he was disapointed that he had missed Such an oppurtunity of exercising his power.

The 2 who had thus obtained his freedom were young men of a promising countenance, So we entered into conversation with them with considerable freedom. They both Seemed inclined to favour us as far as possible, in consequence of which we Resolved to have a warm Dinner if it were possible. On mentioning our wish to them, one of them went Out & Returned with a decent Looking Scotch Woman along with him who, he Said, would Get us anything we wanted. We asked her what She could Get at the Shortest warning. She Said a *Mutton chop*. Well then, a mutton chop be it. In About half an hour She brought in a table, knives & forks etc & in another She brought what we were thinking a Great deal more Long for, viz. the Mutton chop, which was a Very Good one; at Least, She Said So.

While we were eating Dinner, Some of them happened to name me, which She observed & asked me If I was from Belfast, or if I was acquainted with a Clergyman of my name there. I told her I was, Upon which She began to tell us a melancholy Story of how Long it was Since he had married her & what misfortunes had befell her in consequence of it, and ended by Saying that as I was a friend of his, She would treat me to a Jug of Punch, for, Said She, the Good man would take nothing from us though we knocked him out of his bed.

After we had Drank the Punch, we asked her what was her charge. She Said, with all the composure of a Slave, that She would only charge

us one Shilling each, tho it was as well worth Eighteen Pence, as a Ram
was a rarity. One of the Yeomen with whome She was acquainted Said
he would Leave the money for [her] & while he was doing it the other
went out. When he came in, he Said that the People of the Inn had
offered him Dinner for any number he pleased at Eight Pence a piece,
&, Said he, you Shall pay her no more. Upon which, She Got into a terrible passion & Swore She would complain to the Officer. He offered
her 8 Pence Each, which She tossed out of his hand, Swearing that She
would not take 11½d. We now interposed and would have paid her her
charge, but they would not allow us, and on her refusing the money
again, they Very Cruely kicked her down Stairs & threw her table after
her. Lest She would Go to the Officer & make a noise about it, they
took the Lead of her & the consequence was that they were Ordered to
pay her nothing, nor to allow us to do it. However we found means to
pay her before we went to bed, as the yeomen were both So Drunk that
they did not know what they were about.

I must, however, do them the Justice to Say that they Payed for all
that was broughin [*broken*] & before we began to Dinner one of them
Sent to his father's for a parcel of Straw & Blankets, on which we Slept
Very comfortable. But it had been better for us that we had wanted
either his Bed or Pannet, for we Slept So Sound that the Soldiers Stole
all the Provisions that we had Laid in for the next day's journey. For our
rout[e] Lay through Such an unhabited Country that we were told that
we would not Get any thing either to eat or Drink till we would arrive
at Waterford, then Distant about 20 miles.

We were wakened before Day Light, which was the time we missed
our Stock, but as there was no person up, and as we had had Lawful
warning, the Officer Oblidged us to proceed, fasting as we were. Our
yeomen were Sound asleep when we left them, So we could Get no
assistance from them. By the time that it was proprey [*properly*?] clear,
we were two miles out of town. The Capt., who had been in front, fell
back to us & asked us if we had ever heard of Castil— (I do not recolect
the name he Gave it).[37] Then, Said he, 'you will See one of the Largest
Buildings that ever was in Ireland as Soon as you turn the Corner before

you. It was the Only place in Ireland that held out any Length of time against Oliver Cromwell and as Soon as he Got possession of it, he nearly Destroyed it. The Ruins of it now cover About 2 acres of ground. As Soon as we come up to it, you Shall Stop & Look at it.' We thanked him for his information & he proceeded forward to Give orders for the halt.

This wonderful Structure is Situated on a Rising Ground & in what appears to have been the rear is an eminence resembling your Motes, but is wider & not So much of a roundish form as those in your Neighbourhood are. On the top of the eminence is a turret or pillar erected of an amazing height, from the top of which the Capt. told us they could See 20 miles around. There is still a Considerable part of this Stupendous fabrick Standing, which far Surpasses any thing of the Sort I had ever Seen or indeed imagined to be in Ireland.

We Stopped about 20 minutes and Just as we began our march we Saw a horseman coming after us full Speed. The Guard were a Good Deal alarmed & ⅔ rds of them formed across the road fronting the Town, with Charged bayonet. It proved to be only a false alarm ocationed by one of our Yeomen who, on awakening, were told of our having Lost all our provisions & he immediately knocked up Some person, with whom he was acquainted, & having Got Some bread, Cheese & Whiskey, he had mounted his horse & Galloped after, as he Said he could not think of us being Starved all Day through his negligence. The Capt. was not well pleased, but did not Say much. So having Got [our] Store of provisions we proceeded on our Rout[e].

In all this day's march we did not See the least appearance of cultivation untill we came within a few miles of Waterford. The Country was rough, rather hilly and Covered with heath, Among which we could Sometimes See a Little hut not much better than a Good pigs Sty, around which were hundreds of as fine Cattle as I ever Saw. But not the Least appearance of cultivation; Not So much as a potatoe ridge.

We came in Sight of Waterford about an hour before Sun down. The evening was fine & the prospect before us butiful. The town is Large & [there were] a vast number of Ships Lying at the Key, which is So Good that Vessels of 400 Tons can run along Side without discharging any part of their Cargo. The Town Stands on the River Suir, over which is a very handsome Wooden Bridge erected which adds Very much to the beauty of the Town. I can not tell you the exact Length of the bridge, but it appeared to me to be nigh as Long as the Long Bridge of Belfast. On the side next the Town is a Draw Arch for to Let the Shipping pass, the frame of which they Latterly converted into a Gallows, which Saved them the Double Expence of errecting a Gallows & making Graves for the unfortunate Victims, for as Soon as they were died, and Some Say Sooner, they cut them down & Let them fall into the river. As we passed through we were Stopped & the convenience of the place explained to us by the Officer on Duty.

We were marched to the Market house which, having first been made a barrack & then a prison, did not make a Very promising appearance. On entering it we found that it had been used even more than that of Newtown Ards. The East Devon Militia were doing duty in the Town, who rec[eive]d us with three cheers, which was Sufficient to Deter us from asking any favours from them. We had not been five minutes in our new habitation till an Old woman come in to Sell Milk. Her we prevailed on to Go and buy us Some bread, So we had a Good Supper & the Old woman promised to call in the morning & bring us our breakfast. The Market house being Situate on the Side of the Green, & all the Windows [having been] taken out & Iron bars Substituted, could not be Supposed to be Very warm, and as they would not allow us any fire, we were Oblidged to walk backward & forward to keep ourselves warm. Some of our men went down to the Guard house, which was below Stairs, But Dickey, Adams, Stone, McNeight and I walked it out till morning.[38]

[When] the people began to Stir about the Street, then we took post at the windows to See what Sort of people the Waterford folks were. Before we had been Long at our post, there were a perfect croud about the Street, So we Judged it prudent to Sound a retreat as they had So far the advantage that we began to fear being blown up in our camp. We retreated into a little closet which, tho not Very clean, yet we thought

that it would Serve as a [refuge from?] curiosity. We had Just finished
Breakfast, which our Old Woman was punctual in bringing, when a
number of Quakers made their appearance & began to Scrutinize into
everything that they could about the people who were out, &, not Satisfied with this, they came to our closet & on opening the door the first
thing that presented itself to us was an Orange ribbon as a Chain to a
Lady's watch. 'Friends,' Said one of them, 'what makes thee Shut thy-
selves up in this uncomfortable place? Art thou afraid to Shew thy-
selves? If So, thou must be Terrible Offenders and I Sincerely pity thee.'
As he Seemed to Direct the latter part of his discourse to me, I thought
myself bound to answer him. 'No, Sir, we are neither Afraid nor
ashamed to Shew our Faces, but we wish to avoid the Sight and Insults
of Such Detested Traitors as you are. Tho true we are prisoners, but yet
we have our Rights, on which we are resolved that neither you nor any
of your infamous faction Shall Intrude on without proper authority, and
this closet is at present part of that Right. You will therefore please to
withdraw yourself from a place where you have no business whatever
& Leave us in Quiet possession of what is our Right. We wish not to
insult & are determined not to be insulted with impunity.'

   At this moment the Captain who had the command of our Guard
the day before made his appearance, attended by Several Officers. He
had heard part of what I Said, So asked what was the matter. 'Nothing,
Sir,' Said I, 'but these Gentlemen & Ladies are come to See what Sort
of people the United Irishmen of the North are & I am Sorry that our
present Situation puts it out of our power to Give them a proper Idea
of their Spirit. We have now, Sir, Travelled near 200 miles & have never
been Insulted till this morning; that this Gentleman did it' (Saying
which I laid my hand on his Shoulder). 'We are mostly Young men who
have not Seen much of the World. We have Seen So much of it, however, as to know when an insult is intended, but we little thought that
an Inhabitant of the Town of Waterford would be the first to insult people who had it not in their power to return it. You, Sir, have witnessed
our behaviour Longer than any other Officer Since we Left Belfast.
Have we under your care acted imprudently? Do you think we are

deserving of the treatment that this Gentleman has given us? If you Say we are, we Submit, but if not, then we expect you will use your authority to have him turned out of a place where we think he has no business.'

I Spoke So fast that he had no Oppurtunity of interrupting me till I had finished when, Turning to the Brotherhood, he asked them what brought them there. The one who had before addressed us Said that, Seeing there were prisoners in the house, they had asked the Serg^t· for Liberty to come & See them, and on finding these men Shut up by themselves, had asked them the reason. In consequence of which, the young man who Spoke to you last ordered us about our business, telling us we had no business here. Now, we are inhabitants of Waterford & pay for the Keeping of a market house in it & we do not think that any prisoner has a right to order us about our business. 'I think', Said the Capt., 'I have a right. I am Sure I have the power & if you do not immediately Leave, then I will Set you on the Hulks for daring to insult prisoners who are under Guard of his Majesties forces.'

The poor Quakers now made their exit Quick time & we thanked the Captain for the favour he had conferred on us. 'Go out & walk about,' Said he, '& don't be afraid of any of the people who come here. Serve them all as you have these & you will not be troubled with many Visitors.' We took his advice & Six of us arm in arm began our travels, determined that the person we would Give way to must either be possessed of proper power, or treat us in a different manner from which the others did. The plan being made, we walked in a Circuitous manner So as to ocupy the whole area.

We had not walked Long in this manner when a Gentleman & 2 Ladies entered the rooms. They stopped with their backs against the Door & when we came oposite Saluted us kindly, in consequence of which we Quit walking & went to one of the windows. 'Do not Let us interupt your walk,' Said the Gentleman; 'we wish not to disturb you.' We Said we had not stopd walking Since we Left Thomas Town and of course were pretty tired. The man drew near & asked us Generaly how long we had been prisoners, how we had been treated etc. 'How did you Sleep Last Night?', Said one of the Ladies. 'Just as you Saw us when you entered,' we replyd, 'for on acc^t· of the cold, we did not Lye down.' A Serv[an]t now made his appearance, to whome the Gent. whispered Something & he immediately went out again. 'Would they not allow you fire here?' 'No, Sir; we asked & were refused.' 'Well, you have one comfort at Least; you will not be Long here & I hope you will find the place where you are Going better than this. One thing I would recomend to you: to purchase every thing that you think you will want before you leave this [place], as they will make you pay double for every thing you Get there.' We thanked him, but Said we did not know what we Should want. 'A Tin & Spoon are two articles which you can buy here for 1 Shilling & there they will make you pay four for them. These are things you will find the want of immediately, therefore I would advise you to take them with you.'

By this time the Serv[an]t returned with a basket & Set it down in the window. The eldest of the 2 Ladies took a napkin off the basket, Saying She hoped we would not be offended with her for Sending for a Small refreshment for you, as I know that you will find it Difficult to get any thing comfortable here & although this is not the most comfortable dinner you could Get, yet it is the best we could Get in and is nothing but a few Cakes & Wine. We made no ceremony but helped ourselves. After we had done, they asked us if there had been no other person into See us this morning, on which we told them what had passed between us & the Quakers. 'I am Very Glad you Served them as you Say, for they make a practice of Visiting all the prisoners that come in and if they can pick anything out of them, they Go to the Commanding Officer & tell him.' Seeing a number of Officers Coming toward the Market house, they bid us Good by, Saying that if they could Get [permission] they would come & See us in the evening. But we Saw them no more.

That night we Spent in the Same manner we did the preceeding One and at nine in the morning we were ordered to prepare for marching. Our Guard Consisted of the yeomen of the Town, among whome I met with One of the name of Stewart, who Said that Wm. Stewart of Newtown Ards was a friend of his & that he intended to Go and See him the ensuing Summer. They treated us Very well, which was more than we expected from them, as they have by no means a Good character in the Country.

As Geneva is but 9 miles distant from Waterford, we were at the Gate by 3 OClock. We had Some difficulty to Gain admission, owing to the Rout[e] not being Sent with us. At length, however, the Capt. who escorted us prevailed on the Guard to receive us & the Gates were Opened with as much precaution as if there had been an Enemy blockading the fortress. We were marched to the Fort Major's Door, who in the course of half an hour condescended to Visit us. The first thing he did was to arrange us in proper Order, beginning with those who he thought were from Belfast. He placed us on the Right and then asked us if he had been deceived, or whether there were any of those he had picked out that were not from that [town]. As he had picked out an Orange Man who belonged to Newry & whome we did [not wish to be associated with?], we told him there was one that was not from that place. 'Well then,' Said he, 'this must be he', Saying which he turned the poor Orangeman into the ranks again. Then calling to Serg^t. Howard he ordered him to take us to the Belfast Barrack. 'You will See Some of your Countrymen there, who will be Glad to hear from their friends.' Before we reached the Door of our Barrack, I Saw Boyd[39] & Purss[40] Looking out of the window & as Soon as they Saw us, So many others flocked to the door that the Serg^t. was not able to open it, in consequence of which he was Going to put us in the Black hole all night. As Soon as the people inside heard what he was Saying, they all retreated to their own rooms & we were Admitted to enter.

I Shall not Attempt [to] describe the melancholy pleasure that we mutualy experienced at meeting in Such a place, as you will be better able To Judge of it from your own Ideas than from any thing I could Say on the Subject. It was Past their Dinner time, So we Sat down to dinner, which consisted of Soup, Allais Broth, Beef, Potatoes & Bread.

I Shall now endeavour to Give you as Just a representation of the place of our confinement as I can. The Ground, Enclosed by an 18 feet wall, was about Twelve Acres directly Square & at each corner

was a position now converted into coal yards. In the Centre of the
Square, fronting the Sea, was a Large Gate, on the outside of which,
at the distance of 10 yards, was Che Va De Frize[41] errected, between
which and the Gate the Guard was placed. At the distance of 12 yards
from the wall Stood the Barracks, the 4 Sides of which were divided
in the middle to allow the men to pass to the Pumps etc which were
in the rear. 1 of the Sides the Officers occupied, 1 we occupied, 1½
the Soldiers & the other half was made into 2 hospitals, one for the
Soldiers & One for the Cropeys. In the open oposite the Gate was the
market, the back Ground from which to the Extremity of the Cul-
prit's Square was closed in with railing 6 feet high, Spiked on the top,
and into this Yard we were put at eight oclock in the morning. At 11
we came in to breakfast. As Soon as we had finished which, we were
turned out again till Dark, Leaving in each room 1 Man to buy provisions & another to Cook it. The rooms were allowed to contain 18
men. Our pay was 6^d per day, 2^d of which we rec[eive]d in bread, So
had but 4^d to buy every thing else we wanted. Beef was 3^d per lb &
potatoes 4^d – 5^d per Stone, Cabbage 3^d – 6^d per head. We made out
to Save 3^d – 6^d per week, which was Sufficient to receive our Letters,
but if we Got none before Saturday morning it Served to Get a Quart
of Beer & I have Seen 4 of us Sit 3 hours drinking it & it was by no
means uncommon for 6 to throw in ½^d each in order to Get into the
Canteen out of the Cold, for there was no house we could Go into in
the Yard but itself, blow what [the] weather would.

Notwithstanding the friendship & kindness with which we were
treated on our march, yet on my arrival in Geneva I had but 2 Shillings
out of the Guinea I Got in Newry & 13 Shillings pay that we rec[eive]d.
Some people might think that we had been Very extravagant on our
march, as it appears that we laid out 4 times the Sum during our march
that we rec[eived] in Geneva, out of which we were able to Save 3^d per
week. But you who are acquainted with the disadvantages that a prisoner lies under; who is Obliged to Send a Soldier for everything he
wants; will believe me when I Say that we lived much better in Geneva
than we did on our march.

For a considerable time before our arrival, the prisoners had been Guarded So Strictly that they had lost all hopes of ever being able to make their escape, but as Soon as it became certain that we were to embark, we Set every other consideration aside & resolved to attempt it, as we thought that if Only One could make his escape at the price of the Lives of 6 of his fellow prisoners, it would be a cheap purchase. The Officers, however, had always more Suspicion of the Belfast prisoners than any Others. Of course, we were Stricter Guarded.

The first man that made his escape after I went there effected it by having a Suit of Gentle Cloathes Brought him, with Boots, Spurs, Whip etc, in which he equiped himself in the necessary & then walked out & after taking a turn or two in the Square, he came to the Gate & the Officers let him out without the Least hesitation. A few days after this, when we went into the coal yard for coals, one of the men who was acquainted with the Situation of the place ran out on the top of the coals & hopped over the wall, & before the Guard could Get round by the Gate, he was out of Sight. Before this, they had placed a Centinel in front of each Barrack door & they now placed one in the rear of our one.

A few nights after which, 14 men made their escape out of a barrack at the other extremity of our Square. It was one of the Severest nights of rain, Thunder and Lightening I ever Saw in Ireland, So that the noise they made in Setting aside the Iron Bars of the windows was not heard by the people in the next room. At the rear of our Barracks were Sheds in which the Serg^{ts.} Lived, the roof of which was Just as high as our windows, So that travelling down them they had but 7 feet to leap from the eve of the Sheds to the Ground. With Some timber which they found in the yard, they Got to the top of the wall & with their Sheets they let themselves down. The next day, the Snow came on So that they could not make any Search after them.

The next that attempted to make their escape were three men who had the priviledge of Living with one of the Serg^{ts.}, who was to lock them in in the evening. But they conspired to Get him drunk & Stole the Keys of one of the Coal yards & leaped over the wall. Unfortunately 2 of them Broke their legs in the attempt & after cripling along for about a mile they were oblidged to Stop at a House for help, the Good man of which Very Humanely carried them back the next morning; & before the Doctor even Looked at the Broken Legs, they Got each their Hundred Lashes.

They now determined to deprive us of our Cloathes, as they thought that we could not So redily Screen Ourselves in the Country if we Should even Get Out. In consequence of this, they first published a Manifesto calling on the people to use their endeavours to take Such as had made their escape & offering a reward for any that would be taken hereafter, with threat of fire & faggot ag[ain]st any that would harbour any of us.

There were a number of Tradesmen of us at work (Masons, Carpenters etc) & Thinking that they [had] assisted the men who made their escape with Tools, they put them all into one Barrack. As they had always plenty of money, we thought this a favourable oppurtunity of attempting to make our escape in a body. Accordingly, we laid the following [plan?] to effect it. It was agreed that the working men Should by every means in their power Ingratiate themselves with the jailers & Endeavour to find out Someone that would agree to assist us, for which we were to Give them Thirty Guineas & 10 Watches. They Soon found one that they thought answered their purposes & on telling him what they wanted, he told them that he would be on Guard the next day and that he would find means to be planted on their Barrack at 11 OClock: 'And it will be easy for you to break open your door in a few minutes & when you are out, one part of you must endeavour to Secure the Centry in the rear of the Belfast Barrack, while the other [part] breaks open the door of the Coal yard, from which you can hop or let yourselves down by ropes.' This was directly what we wished & accordingly the Tradesmen Supplyd us with Instruments to Set aside the Bars of our windows.

In the room, however, from where we must make our exit was a Soldier confined & how to do with him we did not know. At length, we realised that we Should by every means in our power endeavour to frighten [him] out of that room, if not out of the Barrack. Accordingly, as Soon as he went to Bed we threw 2 tubfuls of dirty Water about him, which had like to have drowned him, upon which he Got up & made Such a noise that the Serg^t. who had Charge of us & who lived in one of the under rooms, came & without asking any Questions had him Sent to the Black hole. We thought this a Good beginning & now waited with anxiety for the ensuing night, which we hoped would Give Some, if not all of us Liberty.

The next day we were busy in preparing every thing for our departure & as Soon as we were locked up at night we began to dress ourselves in whatever cloathes we thought best Suited us. At eight OClock we had all to turn into bed, which we did with our Cloathes on & as Soon as the Roll was called & the Lights out we Got up to watch the Guards, Lest they Should have heard any thing of our intentions. All continued Quiet & on the Relief Going for 11, every man Seized the weapon that he intended to take with him. It was now a second past 11 & we were all Standing round the window when we were Alarmed by a number of Shots, which continued for Some minutes. Had the Shots been Levelled at ourselves, I am certain none of us would have been more alarmed than we were at that inst[ant]. Before the firing ceased, the Drums beat to arms. The first men who turned out were placed to the cannon, one of which was planted against our Barrack.

We now concluded that all hope of anything being effected was lost, So agreed to undress & Go to bed, which to Some of them was by no means an easy task, as they had put on 6 and 8 Shirts. From the bed I lay in I could See what was Going on in the Square, but this was not much Satisfaction as we could not tell what was the Situation of our comrades. At length, however, we Saw Some of them a taking to the Guard house, but could not See who & in a few minutes a Company of men marched to our door, the officer of which called to the Serg^t. to get a Light as his fire had Gone out. They were oblidged to Send to the Guard house for it, which Gave us time to arrange our cloathes a little better, in consequence of which, when the officer came in, he found everything in its proper place & we all in bed & Stripped, So concluded that we had been So all night.

We could not, from anything that he Said, know what had happened, So we were kept in the most painful Suspense all night, nor were we relieved from it till the next day at One OClock, when we were led out to witness the punishment of 5 who had been Got with their cloathes on, each of which Got 400 lashes. As Soon as they was finished, they marched us to the door of the Barrack, where there were 3 of our Comrades Lying dead & cut in the most Shocking manner with Swords, and 2 more inside badly wounded, one of which died the next day. While we were here we Learned from Some of the people who had been in that Barrack that as Soon as the Sentry was placed where he expected, he broke a pane of the window out of which they Gave him the money & watches & he told them to begin to break open the door. As Soon as they pressed upon which, they Soon broke away the Irons of the door, which they carried back into the room &, taking up their weapons, they came out. Upon which, the Sentry fired on them & immediately a Company of men who had been concealed in one of the adjoining Barracks issued out & poured their fire on those who had been in the front & who had attempted to Gain the Coal yard. Three of these were killed & two of those who retreated into the house were wounded. As Soon as they Got inside of their rooms, they threw off their cloathes & Got into bed as Quick as possible, the Jaegers[42] firing on them all the while till the Officer of the day (who was an Irishman) came, who exerted his authority & Got them Stopped. He was ordered by the commanding officer to take everyone to the Black hole that he found out [of] his own bed or with any part of his cloathes on; & the five that were punished were all that were found, none of whome, or those Shot, I was previously acquainted with.

The next day they Marched us round the Corps[es] Twice & the third day they had them hang on the Gallows, under which they regularly marched us 2 or 3 times a day for 3 days more, & then they took them down & disected & anatomised them. They now took all our Coats, hats & Smallcloathes from us, in return for which they Gave us Foraging Caps, Round Red Jackets & Grey pantaloons, & those who could not Sell their Cloathes in 24 hours had them burned in the Yard.

To make us the more remarkable, they Cut off all our Hair (or their Hair, for mine bid defiance to Scissors from the day I left N.T.Ards [*Newtownards*]), the smell of which in the fire had like to breed a plague in the Garrison, as the Greatest number that were there, I Suppose, never had their hair cut in their life.

A Short time after this they turned us all into the Yard one day & Requested us to Sign attestations. This we were by no means prepared for, but in a full consultation (of the Belfast Prisoners) it was thought necessary to Comply with the Requisition. The principal Reason for this was that the first party that were Sent off, on being asked, Refused, Upon which they took them out & Gave them 200 Lashes each and on their Enquiry Gave them this choice: whether to take it or Get the Same number over again. The first one asked Refused, upon which they took him out & Flay'd him till he beg[ge]d to be taken down & he would Sign any thing they pleased. Now in the State we were in at the time we were called on, we had reason to expect that they would even use us worse, if that were possible. This consideration made a Large Majority resolve to do it and by their persuasions prevailed on the rest to Comply with their demands. The next thing was to take the Oath of allegiance, which they Swore us to instead of the Military Act oath.

In order to mortify [us] Still more, the Colonel Gave Orders that we Should carry the Coals for the Soldiers as well as for ourselves, but for Some days they did not ask any of the Belfast men. At length, however, a party of the Jaegers Seized 14 of us one day. The first hand that I was put to was a large box that took 4 of us to cary on our Shoulders & as we could not Get up Stairs with it in that Situation, the Serg^{t.} ordered it to be put on my back & He would push me up behind. With a Great deal of Difficulty I Got about 8 Steps up & finding I was able to Go no farther, I told him to call Some of the men to take it down. He Swore I must take it up & on my Saying again that I was not able, he drew his Sword & began to beat my legs with it. At length, Able to bear the weight no longer, and enraged at his Striking me, I raised myself up & threw the Box back on the top of him. Then leaping over him & it, I made out & to the Guard house as fast as my heels could cary me & told the Officer what had happened & that I was afraid that If they had Got me, they would have taken my life. He told me to Go about my business & he would not allow them to hurt me. This was the only time I was asked to cary Coals for these Hessian Cannibals.

A few days after we had been deprived of our Cloathes, the Guard aprehended 2 women coming in to See their Husbands, with Creels of potatoes on their Back, and on Further examination found that they had Cloathes concealed among them for the Husbands. In consequence of which, the Humane Colonel *Scott* of the *Dumbarton Fencibles* paraded all the Military in the Garrison &, having Saluted 8 of the Strongest, He formed the remainder into a Circle & ordered the poor Victims to be stripped naked, their hands tied behind their backs &, in this Situation before their Husbands, tossed them in a blanket for the Space of 10 minutes, then took them to the pump &, after Coating them as he called it, he Drummed them round the Garrison & then, after every man on Guard had given them a *Stripe* with a Rod, turned them out of the Gate. The above, attested by hundreds of Indignant Spectators, will Serve as a Sufficient character of the People with whome we had to deal.

The next Revolution that took place among us was that of forming us into 4 Companies, with 4 Serg$^{ts.}$ & 4 Corporals to each Company. They took the precaution, however, to Seperate us as much as possible. Luckily, however, Purss and I happened to be nominated in the Same Company. The third Serg$^{t.}$ was a Very Smart man, but the 4th. & all the Corporals were no better than as many puppets. From the time we were thus formed, till we embarked, we were not allowed Light longer than 6 OClock. About this time I rec[eive]d a Letter from Eliza covering a 7/7 Piece,[43] but could Get no acc$^{t.}$ of the Other, but that the Postmaster in Passage had Given it to the Due manager, who Said that he had Given the Letter to Some Other Person.

On 19th Feb[ruar]y Hugh Adrain & two more were ordered to be Removed to Dublin by a writ of Habeas Corpus, which was Very much against us as he Served to keep a number of the Belfast Men Steady, who, when he left us, behaved Very poorly. When they arrived at

Waterford they were detained there without having received anything to live on. As Soon as we heard of which, we mustered up a Guinea & Sent it to them. After which we heard no more of them till the 25th, that they were brought back to Geneva, but as they were put in the Guard house we could not See nor hear from them.

The next morning we were knocked up at 6 OClock & every man paraded in the Square, Surrounded by the Dumbarton Fencibles, Hessians, a Troop of Regulars, one of Yeomanry & 6 Pieces of Cannon, and at Eight were marched out of the Garrison. There was about 4 hundred of us & There was as many Thousand Soldiers lining the road from Geneva to Passage.[44] They had a Sufficient number of Lighters waiting, into which we were put, & as we had to proceed down the river to reach the Vessel they had Cannon placed oposite Dunion Fort,[45] least we Should attempt to carry away the Lighters. When we got on board we were all paraded on the main deck & the Roll called.[46] They then put us all down on the third Deck, which was the place alloted for us. They then Served each man with a Hammock & Blanket, in addition to which they Got the Serg[ts.] & Corporals a Hair Mattress & pillow.

We had been 2 hours on board without any of us being allowed to Go on Deck, nor could we Get a Drink of water. At length, there were orders Given that the Serg[ts.] & Corporals Should [permit us to pass up and down?]. On Going on deck I was accosted by Capt. White,[47] who was Capt. of the Vessel (Though he was So Ignorant that he had to employ a Capt. Roberts to Navigate the Vessel), who asked me how we liked our accomodations.[48] 'Pretty well,' Said I, 'but we would like them much better If you had ordered us our Dinner.' 'Why,' Said he, 'have you not Got dinner yet?' 'No, nor breakfast neither,' Said I. 'Hallo, Steward.' 'Ay, Ay, Sir.' 'What the Devil is the reason that these men have not Got their Dinner yet?' 'Hallo, Purser.'[49] 'Ay, Ay, Sir.' 'What the Devil have you been about, that you have not Given the men their Dinner?' 'They have Got their dinner an hour ago,' Said the over Grown Steward. 'Pray, Captain,' Said I, 'what are we to have for dinner?' O, he Said, 'I suppose you want a bottle of wine to put it down, but we will learn you to Substitute Small Beer in its Stead.' 'Well,'

Said I, 'a little Small Beer, or even water would help to put down the Business, But we have been denied both.' 'Did not you Say that these men had their dinner, Steward?' 'Yes, Sir.' 'Well, what the Devil, do you expect more?', Said he. 'We have had nothing', Said I, 'but dry biscuit & we were led to Expect the Same Treatment as the Soldiers & they have Got Butter & Cheese.' Without Saying a word, the Capt. turned to the Steward & Knocked him down, & turning to the Purser [said]: 'Go and make that old Vagabond do his duty.' 'You will have Some butter & Cheese directly,' Said he to me as he walked in[to] the Cabin. 'I Suppose', Said the Purser, 'you think you have acted Very Clever.' 'I have done what I conceived to be my duty.' 'Well, never mind,' Said he, '[it will serve] you little by & by. In the meantime, Go & Get your damned Butter & Cheese.' Notwithstanding his threats, I walked off an inch taller for the Victory I had Gained & Sent Purss down for the [food], thinking it better for me not to intrude on the enraged Steward till he would in Some measure forget the Smart of the blow he had Rec[eive]d.

As Soon as we had divided the Butter & Cheese we began to look ab[ou]t for the best Situation for to pitch our tents in & Concluded that about the main hatchway would be the most airy Situation. So without Saying a word, Purss & I measured that Part of the Vessel which was alloted us & found that that Very place fell to us. So we began & hung our Hammocks. We had Just 4 Hammock lengths to our Company across the Vessel.[50] But the Hatchway took up a g[rea]t part of it, in consequence of which we could Get only 80 Hammocks hung & we had 98 men, & the next day 9 Serg[ts.] etc of the other Company were ordered berths by the Hatchway to be at hand when called on by the Officers, 2 of which were appointed to each Comp[an]y.

As Soon as they had Got proper Sentinels placed, they Called up No. 1 [Company] for an hour and the Rest followed in rotation, but no person was allowed to appear on deck after dark. I can not now recolect what our allowance was, except the Bread, of which we had 12oz. per day, & while we lay in Port we had ½ Gallon Small Beer, which was afterwards changed into ⅙ part of a Quart of Spirits or ¼ Wine per

[day]. Soup was the principal of our food after Bread, then Burgoo[51] & as for the Butter & Cheese, I think that what 12 of us Got in the week you would think a Good deal too little to Send to one of your Men when working in the Moss.[52] Upon the whole, I am Sure that If we had had it, or could have Got it, there was none of us but would have eat double what we had. We were in messes of 12 each and the one that Purss & I were in was as well found as any in the Vessel, excepting in Spirits when we came to Get it Served out, for the Officer made the measure So Small that in Serving our Company there would be a Gallon left & we used to blame the purser's one with being rather old beside.

These considerations caused us to lay our heads together to See if we could not outwit them & after deliberating on it for a whole night, we finally Resolved to draw up a list of Twenty of the most familiar names that we could & Some that would pretty much resemble the names of Some of the Company. These we were to comit to memory, So as to be Able to throw in one now & then when We Saw an oppurtunity & the other [person] was to have a Tin in his hand & to Say that he was below & and had bid him Get it for him. Accordingly, we Set to work & drew up the list & before the Grog was Served out Purss was So perfect in it that he brought off 12 out of 20 names that we had added to our list & many times we drew 20 Shares by the Same means & one day that we had Whiskey We Got 30 allowances, nigh 5 Quarts, but this we kept till we arrived in St. Pierres, of which I believe, all the Irishmen in the Reg^t. drank a little.

We had not been many days on board till I Got acquainted with the Carpenter's Mate, who was from the Neighbourhood of Killeleagh [and] who from that treated Purss, Boyd & I & any others we pleased to ask, to a bottle of whiskey every night as Soon as it was dark.

We Sailed on Saturday evening the 9th. of March, Just as the Sun went down behind the Cloud top'd Hills of Wicklow, having been from 12 OClock till that time attempting to lift an anchor which, having Got foul, baffled every exertion that could be made to raise [it], tho' there were as many of us at the Capstan as [we] could Get. At length they told us we had no mind to do it, which so exasperated Purss & I that we went on deck & Got down every person that we could & in 5 minutes we did not leave a bit of the Capstan [intact] or one of the bars that we did not break. And then they were Oblidged to cut the cable, leaving 30 fathom & the anchor behind them.

The next morning we were out of the sight of land & I, with many more, So Sick that it was with difficulty I could keep my head. At 12 OClock when the Company were ordered up on deck, there was no help for me, So I was obliged not only to Go on deck myself but Purss & I had to turn the whole Company up to have the roll called, which was neither an easy or an agreeable task, as the decks were as dirty as anything possibly could be & 3 out of every 4 Vomitting till their hearts were like to come up. We were oblidged to cut down a number of their Hammocks before it was possible to Get them out & when we had them on deck, they would have made So-truly Acuff [?] Split his Sides to have Looked at them. Indeed, as twas, I could not help laughing at the appearance they made when drawn up in ranks on the Deck.

The third morning we entered the Bay of Biscay about 5 OClock with a Very fresh gale, which by Seven had increased into a perfect hurricane. Hardly Recovered of my Sickness, at 7 I went on deck to See what it was like. I had hardly Set my foot on deck when the main top Mast went by the Crosstrees, which So frightened me that I was Retreating as Fast as possible, But Purss caught me & Swore that, having Got me on Deck, he would keep me there, for, Said he, you will never Get well if you Stay below. The Boatswain Piped all hands & Soon cleared away the [wreckage] & by 10 OClock the Carpenters had another ready, which was Rigged before 3 OClock, & about 4 away went the mizzen mast Likewise, & it was not till the third day afterwards that we Got it reparred, during which time it blew with increased Violence. After it Subsided, the Carpenter's Mate told me that 3 of the knees had dropped out of her Stern.[53]

However we now had fine, moderate weather which Soon began to Get So warm that we could not Sleep under blankets. As Soon as they had Got all things reparred, they put us all down one day rehearsing a false attack, in order to practise the Soldiers & Sailors & amuse the Officers. They now gave orders that the Companys would Get their numbers painted on their Caps, So that none but the Companies allowed might Get up on deck. They now allowed 2 at a time. Purss and I being So Great with the Carpenter's mate, we borrowed the Paint of him &, taking all the Caps in our mess, we put No. 4 on the oposite Side to their own N°·, which [was] 2, So that one & 2 hung up together, & 3 & 4. They had an oppurtunity of coming on deck when they pleased, only taking care to Fold down the [other] number.

The tenth day we were out, about 10 in the morning, there was a Sail espied by a man who happened to be aloft. Immediately, down Chests, up hammocks; Drum beat to arms & all the prisoners turned down but the Serg[ts.] and Corporals, who were Kept up to throw the dead over[board] Should they come to action. We tacked & bore down on her & chased her all night and all the next day, during which time I could not perceive that we Gained the Least on her. But in the evening of the Second day the Wind dyed away and as we were able to Show more cloth than her, we come up with her before morning & on hailing her, found her to be from London bound for St. Kitts. So [we] were disapointed in the expectations that even Some of the Serg[ts.] and Corporals had formed, of Getting prize money.

The next Vessel we Saw was two days before we passed the line.[54] They Served us the Same as before. It was blowing pretty hard & the Old Vessel Tumbled about So confoundedly as to break the lashing of one of the Guns which, running back, broke a poor hessian's leg & in a few minutes A Sea Struck her with Such Violence that every man on deck who had not hold of a rope fell on the deck & the Balls being laid out on the Qtr. deck, one of the hessians fell with his Cheek on them & Smashed it all to pieces. The Vessel was bearing away with bare poles before the wind &, although we hailed her in English and all the languages of the continent, yet we could Get no answer from her that we could understand. She showed Hamburgh colours So we let her pass.

The evening before we passed the line the Sailors asked the Character of all the Officers. We Gave them all Good Characters but one.

Well, Said they, we will make him Repent his treatment of you before
he is many days older. The next morning they had a Tent errected on
the forecastle, into which they would not allow any of us So much as a
peep, & in order to keep off the officers, they planted 4 Tars [as] Sentries with handspicks, with orders to knock every person down who
would Cross a Chalk [mark] which they made at the Distance of 3 feet
round their Tent. At the Same time they proclaimed by Sound of trumpet that as they were about to receive a Visit from old Neptune, no person Should dare to disturb them in their Preparations. At 12 OClock
all was ready & the Capt. [was] on the poop, with his Trumpet in his
hand, ready to answer anything hailed by the august Personage that they
expected on board, who hailed from his hiding place &, on being Satisfied where we were from, where bound, & what was our Cargo, he
Ordered the Capt. to heave to till he was come on board. As Soon as
the Vessel was hove to, the Curtain drew & he issued forth with his
Lady in a triumphal Car drawn by 8 noted men, whose bodies were
painted in a fantastical manner. As Soon as the Capt. & Officers of the
Vessel had paid their Respects to Mr. & Mrs. Neptune, They asked
them how they dared to pass through their dominion without their Liberty. The Capt. began to appologise for the Liberty they had taken. 'No
appologeys, Sir, I will receive none. Officers, do your duty.' Ten officers now came forward carrying a large tub, which they Filled with
dirty water & placing a round Stick across, they told their Master that
they waited his Orders. 'Hallo Barber.' The Barber Stepd forward with
his Razor in one hand & his Leather in the other. The Razor was an Old
Iron hasp ab[ou]t 18 inches long, cut like a Saw & the leather [was a]
hose. [He had] a water bucket filled with Tarr & every dirt that could
be Got on board. 'As for you, Capt., you are already free of our dominion, So you will please Give place to your first Lieutenant. Constables,
Seize that Vagabond & you, Barber, let this remind you of your duty.'
Saying which, he Gave the Barber a Sound lash with his whip. The
Lieut. was seized & placed on the tub, but on Saying that he wanted to
kiss the Sweet lips of Neptune's lady they released him. After many
compliments to her Good whip, he presented to her a Guinea &

ordered his Servant to take a Doz. of wine to the Tent, in consequence of which they let him off with only one cut with the Razor & a Bucket of water about his boots.

They now began to [concentrate on] the Seamen, 6 of whome they almost drowned, after which the purser was called on, but could not be found. After Searching near ½ an hour for him, they found him under an old hogshead, which he had cut the head out for the purpose. When they Brought him on deck, they had the wrong Side of his wig foremost, than which I never Saw a more condemned looking corpse. 'Fill up that Bason, Officers. That old Vagabond looks as [though] he had neither been Shaven nor his head washed this month. Barber, Strop your Razor, least you Should cut off any of the pimpels on Those Fat cheeks that are blown like 2 bladders by Drinking the Grog & eating all the Fat mouthfuls that Should be Served to the men.' They now tied up his eyes, after which they placed Ropes all across the Gangways, then put a Swab round his neck instead of a towel, with a few Strands of which they choaked him till he opened his mouth, when the Barber, ready with his brush, crammed his mouth as full as an egg of his lather & then Scraped him till the blood ran over his chin.

While the Barber was performing his office, all the rest had Got either Pails of water or Swabs & as Soon as he had finished, they Soused him in the water, hair, head & ears, & then threw the Swabs on the top of him, from which he could not extricate himself for a considerable time. Nor he durst not open his eyes & every time that he attempted to call out, the Barber heaped more Lather into his mouth. At length he Got himself freed from the Swabs & out of the tub, but they kept throwing the water So fast on him that he could not See the ropes, which tripped him 4 times before he got on the Qtr. Deck, from where he went down to his berth.

They now called on the Hessian Colonel, who Stipulated with them for the whole of his Officers, So they had only a few cans of water thrown on them. They next called for the Officers who had charge of us, all of whom paid them handsomely, but on calling for the Officer that we had recomended, he could not be found. Neptune Swore he would not allow the Vessel to proceed an Inch further till he was found; So [he] detached his constables to look for him, who pulled him out of his Chest. As Soon as he was pulled out he Drew his Sword, declaring he would not allow any Vagabonds to use him So. But one of the constables with his handspick Smashed his Sword into a Thousand pieces & then dragged him on deck, to the Joy of every Soul on board. He applyd to the Colonel to use his authority to Save him from the Affront about to be Offered him, which So incensed Neptune that he began to belabour him with his whip. He then offered him [Neptune] a Crown: No. Then half a Guinea: No. Then a whole one: No. 'You have detained me from Dinner this half Hour & you Shall pay for it with a Vengeance. Officers, & you Barber, do y[ou]r duty.' Notwithstanding all his outcries & Strength, they tied up his eyes & placed him on the bason. One of the men poured a little water down his cheek, on which he Gave a Shout & the Barber Crammed his brush full into his mouth & ramed it half down his throat. He held the brush with his teeth till the Barber called for the Stay Tickle to pull it out, upon which he Loosed his Grip. After he had lathered him properly he pulled his razor, but thought that it was not in order to Shave a person of Such Quality as he was now about to do, So he called for his Hone to Set it, Upon which the Carpenter Gave him one of his files, with which he Sharpened the Teeth of his Razor till he was able to cut the Side of the bason with it & then began to scrap[e] the poor Lieut. So unmercifully with it that I was Sorry that I had any hand in Giving his Character. The men treated him worse than the Purser & the worst of it was that his whole Suit was Spoiled & he had Not another.

As Soon as they had finished, Neptune rose & Seated his lady on his Seat & took hers & She called up three of the Sailor's wives who had not been [a]cross the Line before, & being all of the Very worst description of women, they ducked them unmercifully. She then called for 2 of the Hessian Officers' wives & notwithstanding all their & the Officers' remonstrances, they had to be Shaven; & Although they did not duck them, yet they threw as much water on them as wet them as much as if they had.[55]

They had now finished & Upon a Signal from Neptune every Sailor prepared himself with a bucket of water & as many as could Get [there] without Giving the alarm went aloft & upon a Signal from the Boatswain, one of the men called out: 'A Sail — an Enemy.' This brought out all the Officers on Deck, upon which they Discharged all the water they had on the top of them. Upon which, Neptune and his lady withdrew & we went to Dinner.

A few days previous [to] our passing the Line, the Doctor declared that there was a very bad fever on Board. So he laid off a part of the Vessel for an Hospital & the next morning one of our men was found dead. After prayers was read over him He was Sewed up in His Hammock and a 30lb. Shot put at his head & feet, then laid on one part of the main Hatch & lowered into the water with the Greatest decorum. Just as the hatch was drawn up one of the Hessians came running up & told us not to take away the tackles, for they were wanting. 'For whom?', Said I. 'For mine Frow,' Said the German. 'O, very well,' Said I, 'bring her here & we will ease you of her at once.' I thought he was funning us, which was the reason I answered him So Merrily & ordered the Tackles to be unhooked & the Hatch laid on, which was Just done when he came back carrying the Corps[e] of his Frau on his Shoulder. And on Seeing that the Hatch was gone he Gave a kick with his Shoulder & pushed her overboard without any Shot. Nor did She Sink as long as we were in Sight. As Soon as he lost Sight of her he Set up a most lamentable Cry, which Set all the people about a-laughing, upon which I left him & them.

Two days after this it fell upon Purss & I to see the decks cleaned, which had been neglected both the preceeding ones so [they] was in no very Good condition. As the weather was now Very warm and [there was] Some appearance of our being Visited by a Set of more troublesome Visitors than even Neptune, the first thing we did on Going down was to Strip of[f] all our Cloathes. On Going to the Hospital we found a man who appeared to be in the Very Agony of Death. He had fell out of his hammock & was now in Strong Convulsions on deck. I put on my Cloathes as fast as possible & went to the Doctor. I told him there was

a man below, Very bad. 'Byrne,[56] I Suppose,' Said the Son of Esculapi-
ous. 'Why [have] you run? There is nothing the matter with him, but
he wants to coaks me out of a little more Wine.' 'What then am I to do
with him?', Said I. 'Bring the Vagabond on deck', Said he, '& throw a
few buckets of water on him & I'll warant he'll Get up as fast as any
man on board.'

On Going down again the poor man Seemed if possible to be worse
than before. On telling Purss what the Doctor Said, he told me to Go
& tell [the] Officer & swore that if we did not Look Sharp, that Vagrant
of a Doctor would have us all killed before we would reach land.
Accordingly, I Set off to the Officer on duty & told him. He went down
along with me and as Soon as he Saw the Man, he went & brought the
Doctor Down with him, who ordered us to lift him & Cary him on
deck. But before we had Got him halfway up, he expired in our hands.
This was the first person I had ever Saw die & it would be impossible
for me to tell you how it affected me.

The next morning an Old Soldier who was appointed a Serg[t.] Said
he had been Robbed of 2 Guineas. Though every man on board knew
that he had not that much in the world, in the course of the day I heard
him blame John Greer[57] with the theft, upon which I took Greer's part
So far as to Say that I was persuaded that he never took any of his money
& that I thought that he was Very wrong to blame any person at Ran-
dom. 'Would you not Spake about Such a thing had it happened to
you?', Said he. 'I believe not,' Said I. 'Very well,' Said he & away he
went.

The next morning as Soon as I appeared on Deck I was made pris-
oner & Sent to the Poop. I could not tell what could be the matter, but
I presently began to Suspect the Serg[t.] for it, as I Saw him in earnest
conversation with another, who was Sent away for Sheep Stealing.
Afraid that all was not Going on as It Should be, I asked one of the
Sailors to call the Carpenter's Mate, to whom I told my Suspicions.
'Well,' Said he, 'never mind', So Saying he went on deck & took up a
Rope, which he began to Splice & placed himself behind the 2 Serg[ts.],
who were plotting how they would be able to Get me flogged. At

length the one who had lost the money Said he would Go & Get me Released, as he could not See any way that he could hurt me. 'No,' Said the Sheep Stealer, 'rather than that I will Say that I heard him Say that he knew of a man in the Vessel who had Stolen Goods & that he would not inform on him, lest he Should be flogged.'

They now went to Dress in order to be ready when called on to prosecute. As Soon as the Officers appeared, I beged of the Capt. of our Comp[an]y to have me tried immediately, in consequence of which there was a Drumhead Court Martial Called & the 2 Serg^ts. prosecuted with the Greatest Sincerity. I had no hope but that the Court would forgive me, as I did not know what the Mate had heard till he Stepped forward & told the Officer that presided that he had Got Something to Say in the prisoner's defence, & immediately told what he had heard pass between them. The consequence of which was that I was liberated & them Severely reprimanded.

The next night Purss Swore he would make the Sheep Stealer repent what he had Done. He was one of the Serg^ts. who had been placed in our berth & had his hammock next to the hatchway of the main hold, with Purss & I on the Other Side of him. Purss spoke to the Carpenter's Mate & he Said he would assist. Accordingly, he went down to the lower hold & Left all the Hatches open & before Purss went to bed he untied the Ropes of his [the sergeant's] Hammock from the beam & made them fast to the head of his own, So that he could cut him down without any Suspicion. And the Mate Said he would take care to be at hand to throw him down the Hatches.

They purposely kept me ignorant of all the Scheme till about 12 OClock at Night when Purss waked me & we began talking So loud as to wake the Sheep Merch[an]t, who began to remonstrate with us for talking So loud. As Soon as Purss had him properly awakened, he took me by the hand & Gave me a Squeeze & at the Same inst[ant] cut the Lanyard of the other's hammock & down he went to the lower hold. '*Murder, Murder, Murder*,' Shouted Purss. The Mate lepped down to his own berth, which was below us, & Got a candle. '*Murder, Murder*,' Said the Mate. Every one of us now Got up & picked up the poor Devil, who was badly bruised by the Fall but no bones broke. The Mate Shouted for a tickle, which he began to belay round his [the sergeant's] middle, calling for the people to pull up the dead Sheep. But an Officer coming put an end to our mirth, for as Soon as he Saw him, [the sergeant] Swore that it was done on purpose, for that one man Stood at his head & cut the Rope & another Shoved him Off down the Hatch. 'Have you any Idea of who did it?', Said the Officer. He Said he had not. 'Well then, Get up & Sleep farther from the Hatch.' The next night Purss & I went into the Mate's berth to Get a Drink, where they told me all about it.

We had nothing remarkable happened us from this time till the Officer's reconning [dead reckoning] was up, Save the death of one of our mess & 3 of the Hessians & another of their women. Our reconning had been up 2 days & no appearance of land when on the 3rd. morning, about daybreak, we were hailed by a frigate who at the Same time Gave us a Shot. Of all the Scenes I had yet witnessed the One that presented itself to View at this time was the most allarming, as the Hessian Guard immediately charged bayonets & drove our men all Down, Beating them in the most Cruel manner with their Firelocks. Luckily for Purss & I we had Gone up aloft to Sleep that morning, So we were Safe. They were in Such hurry & Confusion putting our men down that they neglected to answer the Vessel, but by another Shot She brought them to their Senses. To our Sorrow, however, She proved to be an English Frigate who had under Convoy the West India Fleet. From him we learnt where we were (about 3 days Sail from our destination). We could not See the Fleet & She left us as Soon as She had Satisfied herself who we were.

That day Purss & I had the Charge of Cleaning the decks again. The Carpenter ordered Wm. Patton[58] (one of our men who was a Carpenter by the way) to Turn the Cock & let the Cistern fill with Water for the purpose of washing the Decks. With the Greatest care he accordingly turned the Cock, but forgot to Stop it again. The Vessel had been Very leaky all the Passage insomuch that the Pumps had to be kept Going 14 out of the 24 hours. This afternoon, however, we had been pumping as hard as possible with all the 4 Pumps & Could not Get her dry. At 12 OClock at night Purss & I had to take the Works for 4 hours & after Working as hard as we could with 32 men for an hour, we could not find that the Water Seemed to Get any lower. I then went & Called the Car[penter]'s Mate & asked him for his handle to Go into the Pump Room to See what was the matter. He took up the Lanthern & went down before me and as Soon as he came to the edge of the well he Gave me the light, caught hold of the Rope & threw himself down. But instead of lighting on the hard Boards, he fell over head & ears in Water. He Soon pulled himself up & as Soon Threw himself into the Cistern & Stopped the Cock, Swearing that there was nothing but death for Patton, if not for us all, for, Said he, you will never be able to free this of water, However you may try.

Accordingly, I went up on Deck, called Purss & told him our Situation & what was likely to be the Fate of Patton Should we not be able to pump out the Ship before morning. 'Get a ropes' end,' Said he, '& we'll Soon press as many to the pumps as will pump the tank dry.' He took out his knife, cut about a yard of the First Rope he met with, which he Gave me, & then cut as much for himself. 'Now,' Said he, 'let us make every Soul on Deck Go to the pumps. Take no excuse from Men, Women or Children. Give the Sentries orders not to allow any person to pass them without orders', & Going to the Forecastle we drove every person down & then Set to & double-manned the 4 Chain Pumps, & after pumping an hour the Mate come up & Said that there were now only 2 feet, which was but ½ of what had been in her when we began. He went down & brought up 2 Gallons of whiskey, which he made into Grog, & by the time it was finished with we had her dry, nor did ever one of the Officers know that anything had been rong, but on taking up their heavy Baggage it was all Rather *!!!!!!!*

The next day there was a man kept on our mast to look out for land. About 12 OClock we were alarmed with the Cry of Fire & Immediately found that the Galley had Caught Fire, but the Place being all covered with Shot Iron Prevented the Fire from Spreading. But the chimney taking Fire, there was considerable danger to the rigging. The Officers were all Gathered about Doing no Good & preventing every other person from Getting nigh it, till the Boatswain with a Ropes' end cleared them all into the Cabin & we Soon Got the Fire under [control].

The next day about 8 in the morning [of] 9th. April we came in Sight of Barbadoes, which we passed So close as one of the Seamen from the mizzen Top threw a Buiscuit ashore. About Sun down we anchored in the Harbour of Fort Royal, about a mile distant from the Town, which was right ahead. About a mile above which Stands the Strongest Fort in the Island, or indeed, in the West Indies. On our Larboard Side was another Fort & on our Starboard the Setting Sun reflected its rays on a most beautiful Orange Grove, which extended about ½ a mile in length, behind which was a number of Negro huts. The Very thought of which Chilled my blood, but when I began to think that I was doomed to live 14 years among them, my heart Sickened at the Very Idea. The only thing with which I could console myself was that there was little probability of my living So long.

Purss & I were Just Sitting by Our Selves talking about Such Things when our Old Friend the Carp[enter']s Mate Came to us and asked us what we were thinking of. From the Friend to which we owed So much & of whose disposition we were So well Satisfied, you may Justly Suppose that we withheld nothing. On Telling him what we were talking about, 'I have been Just thinking', Said he, 'that it might be in my power to Serve you. I have before told you that I intended to make my escape from this Ship as Soon as possible. I hope that before She leaves this port, I will be able to effect my escape & if I do, be assured that I will never leave this Island without taking you both with me.' 'And', Said he, 'I would recomend to you to Go to St. Pierre's, as I think that from there you will have a better oppurtunity of making your Escape than from any other [place] in the West Indies.' He bid us Good night & we entered into a new consultation to See what was proper to be done. But being intirely Ignorant of what they intended to do with us, we could come to no decision, but Resolved to keep in View what our Friend had Said to us.

The next morning we were told that we might Volunteer with any Officers on board that we pleased. We at first rejected this proposition with disdain, but on looking at it the Second time we found that it would be for our benefit, as by this means a number of us might Go together, whereas if we were drafted, we Ran a Risk of being all Seperated. In consequence of this Purss & I Reparred to the Acting Adj^t· & Told him that a number of the Belfast People wished to Go with him. He Said he was Very Glad as he had wished to have had 50 of them, but the Commanding officer had refused, Saying that he would not allow So many to Go to any one Reg^t. But on acc^t· of the 43rd· being Very weak, he had ordered that he Should have [the] Liberty of taking 34 with him. We accordingly Set to work & [Hull?]^59 made up his Quantum.

But Some of the men took what we had done amiss & began to Say that we were only doing it to Obtain favour with the Officers, in consequence of which I asked the paper from the Officer & tore it to pieces, telling him at the Same time what was my Reason. 'Well,' Said he, 'they have perfect Liberty; let them Go where they please.' Purss & I, however, told him We were determined to Go & John Boyd Said he would Go along. At length there were 10 people from the north Resolved to Go & the Officer made up the Rest with the best looking men he could find.

Having his numbers completed, he told us that he would Go off directly, in consequence of which we prepared ourselves & at 10 OClock we bid adieu to our Companions & Set out in a Canoe for St. Pierres. But our Vessel proved So leakey that we were Oblidged to Run Ashore in Fort Royal & Charter [a] Ship. This one had Eight oares & Two masts, So we expected to Go a Good Sail. We had a Company of the Jaegers to Guard us. The Negroes who were to take us round were every one naked and the Poorest Set of Boatmen I have ever Seen in that Country. The wind was fair & [there was] a Good breeze, So we expected to Go in Three hours, but our Skipper ran us foul of a Vessel & Getting under his Bowspritt we carried away both our masts, So that the poor Blacks had to take to their oars, Some ag[ains]t their will. As Soon as they Began to Row, one of them began to Sing; as he was tired, another began & frequently they [blew?] into horns, which had a Very Good effect.

The Beauty of the Prospect as we passed from Fort Royal to St. Pierres far exceeded anything I had either Seen or had any Idea of. In every little Val[le]y, of which there are a prodigious number, there was a plantation [at] the Bottom of the Vale planted with Plantain Trees, the leaves of which were 6 feet long & 2 broad and on each Side of the Banks the Negro huts [were] arranged in straight lines. At the base of each [were] a number of Fruit Trees, loaded with Fruit Such as Oranges, Limes, Saursap, Guave, Sugar Apple, Mungos, Mammy Apples, Alligator Pears, Cocoa Nut & Cabbage Trees, all of which they arrange in Such order that they run above each other as Regularly as the Hill does, except the two last which tower far above the rest & are So much similar that you would not know the difference for Sometime. In all these places, Tho' Nature has laid the Foundation, yet art had almost outstripped her in the Superstructure which, could it but be Viewed without refrence to the Back Ground, it would indeed defy the Pencil of [*MS torn*] to do Justice to it. But allas, when we look into the Back Ground & See 300 or 400 of our fellow Creatures with Small howes tearing up the Ground that had never been entered by the Plough, the eye turns back disgusted, Saying that the former is only Visionary pleasure while the latter is real misery. But be not to[o] hasty; turn your eyes again; perhaps they may have deceived you in the first look. Hark: 1 2 3 4 5 6 7 8 9 lashes inflicted on a poor old Man who has not as much cloathes on him as would cover a pincushion. And for what? The Head of his hoe is loose & when it Should fly off & hurt Some of his fellow Sufferers, [he is punished for it?].

While the Punishment is inflicting, the poor feeble old man Stands errect, braces every Nerve, & Casting his languid Eyes toward heaven Seems to call on the Judge of all the Earth to attest his innocence. Not a word, not a Sigh escapes his lips, though they Should Beat the Flesh in Slices of[f] his emaciated body. Poor miserable Creatures; what a lot is yours in this World, or rather, what will be the Fate of your present tormentors in the Next? Surely it will be more tolerable for Sodom & Gomorrah than for the Inhabitants of these Isles, in that Day when the world & the Inhabitants thereof will be Judged by him who is Able to make manifest the Secrets of all hearts; and not only for them, but for every person who has been concerned in that cruelest of all Trafficks.

Our passage lay all the way close in Shore, So we had a full View of that Side of the Island, which far exceeds any I saw for beauty. We arrived at St. Pierres about 5 in the Evening & on Going ashore we found that the Barrack was in the other end of the Town. We had travelled about half a mile without finding any person that could Speak a word of English, So the Officer Stopped, not knowing whether he was Going Right or not. As Soon as we Stopped, I began to look about me, to See what Sort of people they were that lived in Such houses as I Saw the Town consisted of. The first person that Struck my attention was a Young Lady of Exquisite Beauty, at least I thought her So at that moment. She had come to the Door to Get a better look of us, So I had a full View of her as She played with her Fan. She let it drop: 'Gin, Gin, Gin.' A negro girl come running & lifted her fan. Tom, a black boy, come running. She Said Some thing in French that I could not understand, but immediately the poor Negro began a-crying. The little boy returned with a Small cutting whip in his hand, with which She began to beat the girl in the most unmerciful manner. How long She continued this Amusement I cannot tell, for before She had done we were Ordered off, but I could hear the Shrieks of the Wench as long as we were in Sight of the House. I hardly ever felt more mortified than at that moment. Before I come on Shore I had pictured to myself the Inhabitants Pale, languid &, in Short, every thing that was disagreeable, but the appearance of this Woman deranged all my Ideas & before I was out of Sight of the house I would have been well pleased to have Seen the Island and all its inhabitants Sunk.

I paid no more attention to any person or thing till the party were Ordered to halt. On looking up, I Saw we were in Front of the Barrack, Surrounded by a numerous host of disciplined Murtherers, of which I was Shortly to become a Scholar. I was on the right of the Party and as Soon as the Colonel come He asked me how long I had been inlisted. I answered with Some degree of Indignation that I never had been inlisted. 'How come you [are] here, then?', Said he. 'By Force,'

Said I, 'for had it been left to myself I would as Soon been hanged as consented to have worn a Red coat.' The Colonel passed on without Saying any more to me. He asked them all; Some Said they had been in the army before, but most of our country people Said that they had been inlisted on their arrival in Geneva. When he had done, he turned to our Officer & told him he had brought 34 Rogues & but one honest man to the Reg^t. & 'I am afraid that we will have Some trouble to keep him; however, we will try.'

We were now told off among the different Companies for the Night & unfortunately for me I was Sent with 2 others that I knew nothing about. We were delivered to a Serg^t. who might be about 18 years of age, who took us into a room & told us to Sit down & he would Go & Get us our Supper. We had Soon a Croud of people about us, enquiring who we were, whence we come etc. I presently fell in with a Belfast Woman who told me She was a Serg^t's wife who was also from Belfast, that his name was Kelly. Presently the Serg^t. made his appearance & ordered all the people to their own berths, Then asked me as many Questions as would have kept one all night to answer. [He] Called for a bottle of rum & offered me Some. I took a little & Gave him the bottle, which he Gave to my Companions, who handed it about till it was finished. By which time our Supper was come, which consisted of Bread & Cheese, which they had the Goodness to assist us in eating. In the meantime, every one who could Get a Glass of Spirits Insisted on our drinking with them, but knowing the mottives which actuated them & knowing that it was not in my power, even if I had the Inclination, to Repay them, I Set myself positively against drinking anything but Water. Before we went to bed there was Orders Given that we Should Bathe ourselves in the river every [morning] before Gun fire till further orders. That night I Sat with Serg^t. Kelly, & Mrs. Kelly Looked out for a berth for herself.

The next Morning we were paraded with the Reg^t. & the Grenadier Captain picked out 12 for his Company, among which N^o. was Purss & I.[60] As Soon as we had breakfast we were ordered to Go & Wash all our Dirty Cloathes in the River. This was by no means an easy task, as neither of us had washed any thing on the Passage. The River was full of Black Women for ¾ of a mile up above the Barracks, So we did not like to Go in among them, but went up the river till we were above them all, where we Staid till we were made prisoner for being absent from dinner. We were not put in the Guard house, however, as we pled Ignorance of the Dinner hour. After Dinner we fell in with Mrs. McComb, who told us what we might expect & from whom we experienced many acts of friendship while She Staid.

That night I lay on the Boards & in the morning felt myself Very unwell. However I made no complaint & in the Evening we were ordered to Go to Drill. I had a Very Severe pain in my Head, attended with dizziness. We had been out about an hour when the Colonel came & ordered us to be Fronted to the Sun & our hats Set up, for Said he, till they can look Steadfastly at the Sun without Winking you will never make them like Soldiers. We Stood in this position about 20 minutes & as Soon as we were put in motion the diziness increased So much that I fainted. The Serg^t. ordered Some of them to put me up & as Soon as I was Sensible of what was Going on the Colonel Swore I was Drunk, but he would Soon find a way to put Such tricks as that out of my head. 'You must drink less tomorrow,' Said he, 'or I will put you in a place where you will Get nothing but bread & water.' 'I wish I was there now,' Said I, 'for I would rather have a mouthful of Cold Water now than all the Wine or Spirits in the Island.' 'Take him to the Barrack,' Said he.

Two of the men were turned out who went along with Me to the Barrack, where Some of the Women Got Limes & Rubbed my Temples with [them] & Gave me Some of the Juice to Swallow, which recovered me a little. By the time the Reg^t. were dismissed, the Colonel & Doctor[61] called at the Room to See me. The Colonel asked the Dr. if he thought I was Drunk. 'No, Sir, but I am afraid that he is much worse. You have been too much in the Sun,' Said the Doctor, '& if you are not better by tomorrow morning you must come to the Hospital.'

That night Mrs. McComb Got me a Hammock & blanket & I was in [hopes] that a Sleep would have cured me, but in the morning I was

worse, So was ordered to the Hospital by the Serg^t. I was Scarce able
to walk to it & when we Got there the Doctor was not come. I asked
the Serg^t. of the Hospital to let me lye down a few minutes, but he
would not allow me to Go into the inside of any of the rooms. Seeing
Some Goats feeding on Plantain leaves, I went & Drew them away & lay
down on the leaves. I was lying here Sweating when the Surgeon made
his appearance, who on Seeing me asked who I was & what was the
Reason I was not put to bed. 'He is one of the United Irishmen,' Said
the old Serg^t., '& I did not know whether you would allow him to be
put in a room along with the other patients.' 'You did not know,' Said
the Doctor, taking him by the Collar, 'you Rascal, I will let you know
that one man is as Good as another the moment they enter the Gates of
the Hospital. Take & put that man in bed Directly.' The Old fellow took
me by the arm & lifted me up & led me in to the inside of the Hospital, & then left me.

I asked the first person I Saw to let me rest myself on his bed & without waiting for an answer I lay down. The man on the bed took up a
bottle and asked me if I would take a little wine & water. I took the bottle & took a little in my mouth, which I thought did me a Good deal of
Good. I felt myself Quite Refreshed & began to look about me. The
Room I was put into had 24 Beds, 23 of which were then taken up by
as many patients & the 24th I was to fill as Soon as the Old Serg^t. could
find time to bring me bed Cloathes. I took particular notice of all the
people in the end of the room that I was to lye in, to See if I could find
any of my fellow prisoners in it, Several of whom were in before me.
As I could find none that I knew, I threw myself down on my bed without any Cloathes (The Beds have canvass bottoms) & lay there till the
Doctor came in to See us.

As there were Several patients between him & me, I waited to See
how he would treat them. When he came to me he asked the Serg^t.,
with a curse, what was the reason he had not Got a bed made up for
me. He Said he had ordered the orderly to Do it & thought it was done
accordingly. 'Well, then, let that teach you to See that these things are
not neglected in future', Saying which he Gave him a hearty Box on the

Ear. He then took hold of my wrist & after feeling my pulse he ordered his assistant to do the Same. 'Well,' Said he, 'what do you think of that?.' 'That is the Quickest I ever felt,' Said he. The Surgeon now called for bandages & his Instruments. 'I am Going to Draw a little Blood from you,' Said he. 'You will be the better of it. Do you think you will faint?', Said he. 'I believe not.' 'You had better not Get up at any rate,' Said he.

When the bandages etc were come, he took 14 ounces of Blood from me & then ordered me an Emetic. He then went away, telling me he would be back by the time the Emetic would cease to operate. When he come back, he ordered me Some fresh medicine & Gave Strick [*strict*] charge that I Should have nothing to Drink but Toast[62] or [raw?] water & although I was choaking with thirst, yet I could never take neither of these, for before I could Get them to my mouth my Stomach turned at them. Notwithstanding this, I was not to be allowed to Get anything else & he told me If any person would be foolish enough to offer me anything but these, & I be foolish enough to take it, that he would not answer for my life a minute longer.

A few minutes after he left me I was attacked with pains in every Joint in my body. I thought that my whole Frame was pulling to pieces, In consequence of which I tumbled about till I was not able to move myself any longer. Then I asked for a Drink of water, hoping that it would have the Effect that the Doctor Said. But I could not find any person mad enough to give me any, which enraged me So much that I resolved to have some, be the consequence what it would. With this intention I attempted to Get up & none of the Orderlys being near me, I was out of bed before they Saw me, but was So weak that I was not able to Stand & on falling, had like to Dash my brains out against the wall. The orderly men now put me in bed & one of them Sat by me till the Doctor came at eight OClock; & then they told him what I had done & what I wanted. He Told his assistant to Visit the rest of the patients & Sat down beside me. Having felt my pulse for at least 5 minutes, he called for his Instruments. 'I am Going to bleed you again,' Said he. As Soon as they came, he bared my arm & took 5 ounces more from me, Then ordered a man to Sit along with me all Night. I was in hopes of being able to prevail on the man to Give me a little cold water, but in this I was disapointed, for when I asked him to Give me only One mouthful, he only asked me how much it held.

The next morning I felt myself worse every way, but as the orderly Said I was better I dared not contradict him. But when the Doctor came at 12 OClock I told him how I felt & in consequence of my complaining So much of a pain in my head, he ordered them to blister me on the back. I asked how long the Blister was to remain. '24 Hours & you must not attempt to have it taken off Sooner.' I had never Saw a blister, nor knew anything about how it would effect me. Of this, however, I did not remain long Ignorant, for the Serg^t., when he put it on, told me I Should lye on my Back all the time & before I had lain many minutes in that Situation I was perfectly acquainted with the manner that a Blister operates on this frail Body of ours. I had not felt the pain of the Blister long till I was in a Great measure relieved of that in my head, which I thought more than ballanced the other, as there was nothing frighted me So much as the fear of the pain in my head turning into a Delerium, in which Case I knew that I would be likely to Say things that might be attended with Serious effects not only to myself but to my companions.

When the Doctor came in the Evening he Visited me first & asked me how my back was. I told him it was Very Sore, but that my head was much better. Then you had better let the blister remain till morning & by that time I Suppose your head will be well & I will Give you Something to make you Sleep. In this, however, he was not as Good as his word, as I did not Sleep a wink all night. In the morning the Dr. asked me how my back felt. I told him it was Very Sore. 'Have you Stripped it this morning?', Said he to the Serg^t. 'Yes, Sir. I never Saw a finer blister in my life.' Though I was in perfect misery, yet I did not like to contradict him, as I thought that he would do it as Soon as the Dr. would Go away & I knew that If I had, the Dr. would have punished him for his neglect, which would have been nothing in my favour.

As Soon as the Dr. went away I called for him to come & Do it, but he was otherways engaged. So I remained in that Situation till the Dr.

came at 12 OClock & by that time the blister had wrought almost intirely round me. As Soon as he came to me I told him that my back had not been Stripped & that I was in perfect misery with it. As Soon as he heard me he called the Serg^t· & Orderly & told them to Open my Back till he would See it. 'I have Just Seen it,' Said the Serg^t·, '& there is nothing the matter with it, for all the noise that he keeps [on] about it.' The Fire flashed out of the Dr.'s eyes. 'Shall I open it?', Said the Serg^t. 'Dare you disobey my orders?', was the reply. They now lifted me up & took off my Shirt, but did not Get time to take away the blister till he knocked them both down & then Kicked them well for failing. He then called for Some plantain leaves. They had been all Given to the Goat. 'Take them two Vagabonds to the Guard house,' Said he to the assistant, '& Order the first man that you meet to bring Some plantain leaves from the market.' He then put on my Shirt & laid me down again.

When they were Gone he walked back & forward in the room with his arms folded, without Saying a word. As Soon as the man came with the Leaves, he tore one of them off[f] the Stem & taking the Blister off, he applyd it to my back. 'Now,' Said he, 'you deserved to Remain in punishment much Longer for not telling me before, but being a Stranger to the Rules of this house I forgive you.' The leaves had not been long at my back till I fell asleep & when I awakened I had no longer any pain, either in my Head or back, but felt Very weak. When the Dr. came in the Evening I told him I was Very hungry (I had not tasted anything for 4 days). 'I am glad of it,' Said he, 'but you must not eat anything yet a while, as your Medicine will be enough for you, nor [can you] drink anything but Toast Water.'[63] I thought with myself that It would be better to have died with the fever than to be Starved, but as he thought Otherwise I had no Shift but do as he ordered.

The next morning I was considerably worse & The Dr. Swore that I had Got Something more than he ordered, in which he was mistaken. He ordered the assistant to pay particular Attention to me in the Course of the Day & not to allow any person but the Orderlies to come near my bed, which Orders he Renewed at 12 OClock to the Serg^t·, who[m] he [had] released.

In the evening I was worse Still & he ordered the Assistant[64] to take 5 more ounces of Blood from me & to Give me a noggin of Beef Tea before he did it. While the tea was drawing the assistant found means to Get himself Drunk & by the time he came to me he could hardly hold the Lance. The Serg^(t.) tied up my arm & he Cut me in 4 different places, but could Get no blood. I told him that I believed there was Very little left in my body & that [what] little [there] was Seemed to be determined to Stay there. 'Well, try the other,' Said he. On Looking at it, he Swore that if there was but one oz. in my body, he would engage to bring it at the first Cut. He now took hold of the Lance & brought the Blood indeed, but he cut my arm better than an inch. I was So much fatigued with Sitting up So long that I fainted & my arm would not bleed. He called for Some medicine and Gave me that which recovered me & Sat me up again. Then [he] Gave me his hand to Grasp. I was perfectly mad at the manner in which he had Butchered me & as Soon as I Got hold of his fingers I called up every portion of Strength in my body & Gave him Such a *Loving Squeeze* as made him Shout for *Joy* & the blood flew in his face. He pulled out his hand & Called for a plank of wood, Swearing that he would make me repent that before he Stopped my arm. When the piece of wood came I took it in my hand, but I was resolved if possible that I would put a Stop to my Bleeding, as I Saw that he intended to Take more from me than the Dr. ordered. In this, however, I was Disapointed, as the exertions I had made use of in Griping his hand had Such an effect that I was not able to Stop it till he had taken 10 Ounces from me, which he ordered the Serg^(t.) to throw into the Necessary.

In the morning when the Dr. came he found me So weak that I was Scarce able to Speak to him. He asked me what was the matter. I Shook my head. 'Where is that Blood that was drawn from this man last night?' The Serg^(t.) Said he had been ordered to throw it in the Necessary. 'How much was taken from him?' 'I do not recolect,' Said the Serg^(t.) 'My arms are Very Sore,' I Said, & bared my arm to him, which was all festered, [there] not having been anything applyd to the 4 cuts he made in it. 'Show me the other,' Said he. I bared it and he Shook his head & told the Serg^(t.) to Get Some mulled wine for me as fast as possible & in the meantime to Send in Some more Beef Tea & to tell Mr. Cathcart to come in. When the assist. came, he asked him how much blood he had taken from me the night before. 'You ordered 5 oz.,' Said the Cunning as[sistan]t. 'Was I drunk, Sir, that I do not recolect how much I ordered? How much did you take from him?' 'I obeyd your orders & from each of these orifices took an Ounce.' 'I Suppose,' Said the Dr., Shewing him my arms; 'I beg you will never let me See Such a thing again as long as you are in this Hospital.' The Dr. now Ordered Some Salve & put Some on my arms, by which time the wine was come, which he told me to use often but Very Sparingly, as I was too weak from loss of blood to bear much at once.

About 10 OClock 2 men in the next beds died, which Shocked me Very much, as one of them was in a Brain fever & was oblidged to be tyed. At 12 The Dr. ordered me Partis[65] & Toast & in the Evening Tea (which was Continued to me as long as I remained in the Hospital). In about a week after this I was able to Get up & the first Person I Saw was John Boyd, who had been in the fever also but was So much better as to be able to come to my bed as Soon as he Saw me. We were Sitting talking together & to a man who came along with us & who was in the next Bed & Seemed to be Quite recovered, when after a Strugle of a few minutes he Gave up the Ghost.

In a few days I was able to walk about & upon enquiring after the Men whom I had took notice of when I went in, I found there were but 2 of them alive (& before I left it both these died). I had been walking about 3 days when I was again attacked with a return of the fever. The Dr. ordered me a Sweat. The Sergt. brought a number of blankets & put them on me & by the time that the Dr. came at 12 OClock I was not able to Speak to him. He ordered Some of the Cloathes to be taken off & told me that however Severe it had been, it had Compleatly Carried away my fever. When he came in the Evening I was much better & he ordered me a fresh bed etc.

The next morning I Got up again. A few days after this John Boyd relapsed & as a Sweat had been of So much benefit to me, he persuaded Some of the people about him to throw their bedclothes on him &

when the Dr. came he found him much in the Same Situation that I had been in before. But his opinion of him was Very Different, as he Said as Soon as he Saw him that he was killed. Seeing that, I paid more attention to him than he [the doctor] thought was right. He ordered me to be removed to another room & not to be allowed to come in the one where he [Boyd] was, but on Speaking to him, he ordered me to be admitted. I paid Every attention to him in my power; in 4 days, however, he Expired.

After this, I could not content myself in the Hospital, So beged of the Dr. to allow me to Go to the Barrack, which he refused for a week, but Seeing that I was not likely to Get well there, he at length allowed me to leave, Giving me Strick Charge not to do anything till he would order me, [and] telling the Capt. that I was to be Convalescent a fortnight & then to be brought to him.

At This time the Reg^(t.) was So Sickly that the men who were well had to be on duty 2 nights & in bed one. In consequence of this, I was but 4 days out when I was ordered to m[oun]t Picquet on the Governor. It was of no consequence that I told him what the Dr. Said: there was no other Person & the Picquet must be there. We went on at Sun Down & left it at daylight. I was placed Sentry at the Guard house door at 10 OClock and in a little time it began to rain & Thunder in the most Tremendous manner, the consequence of which was that I was oblidged to Stand there till Morning Wet unto the Skin.

When I Got to the Barrack the Serg^(t.) ordered me to Go & Get the breakfast ready, as there was no other person in the Company but myself. I was oblidged to Cook all day & at night to m[oun]t Picquet on the General Hospital, from whence the night before a man had Deserted. The next morning I was oblidged not only to make breakfast, but to Go the wood to Gather Wood. That night I got in bed & the next night [had] to Go to the G[enera]l Hospital again & before morning I was So bad with the Flux that I was oblidged to be assisted to the Regimental Hospital the next morning before day light, where I remained a fortnight & Then went to the Barrack again, pretty well recovered.

By this time my Spirits was So much depressed that I [was] fit for nothing and a State of Convalescence in the Barrack is worse than doing duty, as you have everything to do, Though you were allowed to do nothing by the Dr. I remained 6 days in this State, during which time I neither eat nor Drank anything but a Days worth of milk in the morning, which my friend Singleton Gave me (Milk is 30 Days [*illegible*]). The 6th. Evening a Capt. of another Company took notice of me & asked me what was the matter with me. I told him I did not know. 'If there is anything', Said he, 'that you think will be of any Service to you, name it & if it is to be had in Town I will order it for you.' I told him that I knew of nothing that I thought I could either eat or drink, but the fact was that I durst not take anything from him for fear of offending my own Capt.

The next morning there was to be 4 men punished & I was called on, along with the rest, to See it. The punished [were] in the inside of the room to prevent the Negroes from Seeing them. When they began, they placed us So near the Triangles that [with] every lash they Gave, as Soon as the Skin was cut, the blood flew in my face. Shocked with this, & overcome with the fatigue of Standing So long, I fainted before they had half Done. The Capt. followed me down Stairs & ordered me a Glass of Wine and as Soon as I was recovered, 'You See', Said he, 'what the effects of Misconduct in the Army [are] and as the punishment of another has affected you So much, you had need to take care lest you Subject yourself to Suffer.'

At 12 OClock I was ordered to Go to the wood to Gather Wood to make ready the Dinner. I had made up my burthen & was coming home when I was met by the Dr., who asked me in a Very Surly manner who I was and as Soon as I told him he pulled the burthen off my head & ordered me to Go along with him to the Guardhouse where, when we arrived, he told the Serg^t that I was confined for disobedience of orders. Then, addressing himself to me: 'I do not intend to have you flogged, but I am resolved to keep you there till you are well.' 'I am Glad of it,' Said I, 'for I believe I Shall never Get well in the barrack room.' 'Tis your own fault,' Said he & away he went.

I had not been long in my new habitation till the Capt. happened to pass by & on Seeing me asked why I was confined. I told him that I had been ordered by the Serg^t. to Go & Gather wood & that on my return I was met by the Dr. who ordered me to the Guardhouse for Disobeying the orders he Gave me on leaving the Hospital, Viz. not to do anything or to Go to parade till I would be ordered by him. 'And did you tell the Serg^t. this?' 'The Dr. told him himself.' The Serg^t. was then Sent for and asked why he had disobeyed the Orders of the Dr. in Sending me out in the Sun. He Said he had forgot. 'But you See that the Dr. has not forgot, for he has put this man in the Guardhouse for Going out, although he could not avoid it. Step in & relieve him & you [Bryson] Go to your room.'

Before I Got there I was met by the Dr. 'Well,' Said he, 'I was coming to Liberate you, but I See that Some person has been before hand with me. Who released you?' 'Captain Cameron, Sir.'[66] 'And who has he Confined in your room?' 'The Orderly Serg^t. who Sent me out.' 'And where are you Going now?' 'To the Barrack room, Sir.' 'Well, you must Go to the Hospital in the Evening, for you look worse than when you left it. Don't forget; if you do it will be worse for you than being Confined for Gathering Wood.'

In the Evening I went to the Hospital again & in a fortnight was pretty well recovered. But on Pursses attempt at Desertion & Subsequent Punishment my heart Sickened & in a few days I was worse than ever. The Dr. now Quit Giving me any medicine & ordered the Ward Master to Give me what ever I called for. In this Situation I remained for a Month, Sometimes in bed & Sometimes a cot. The Dr. now began to Give me medicine again & told me if I did not raise my Spirits I would Certainly die.

The next day he by Some means Got into his hand a letter from you & brought it to me at 12 OClock when he Gave it to me. He Said he had brought me a Medicine which he expected would be of more Service to me than any I had yet Got. I asked him what it was. 'Tis a letter from Some of your friends in Ireland; here it is.' I took the Letter from him & put it under my head, Intending to examine it well before

I opened it to See whether the Seal had been opened. 'Why don't you read it?', he Said. 'I thought you were Going to Give me Some fresh medicine before you went away, Sir.' 'Not now, I believe,' Said he, & away he went.

As Soon as he was Gone Down Stairs I took up the Letter & began to Examine it, but could find no Sign of its being opened. But before I had finished my examination he came back again. 'Did you think that I [had] opened your Letter?', Said he. 'I had a Strong Suspicion that It was opened,' Said I, 'but I had not the least Idea that you did it.' 'Well, I hope you have been mistaken in your Suspicions.' 'I believe I have, Sir.' He went away Seemingly not at all well pleased, but I could not find out what was the matter.

However I Soon found out what was wrong, for a few minutes after he went away the asst. came in So Drunk that he could not keep from tumbling over the beds. He came right to my bed Side & asked me if I had not complained to the Dr. at the time He bled me last. I told him I had not. 'You are a D——d Lyer, Sir, & I will have you flogged before you are many days older.' I made him no answer, but turned my face to the wall, upon which he left me & went to a poor halfwitted Ideot which was kept in the Hospital for an Asst. Cook (one of the hopeful Recruits of '96)[67] & ordered him to make him a beef Stake for a Chuk[68] before Dinner. Poor Frank Said that the meat was all passed. 'And why did you not keep a piece for me?' 'Because your mess does not come here,' Said Frank. 'Go to the mess room & Get your Dinner there & not come here every day bothering my people every day & taking away every bit of meat & drop of soup which Dr. Salmon orders to be Got ready for the Sick men.' The Asst. began to laugh at his fury & taking up a large flesh fork, he began to Search out the Kitchen for a piece of beef. But Frank Soon put him out of that by Throwing a ladle full of boiling water about his legs. A proper Scuffle now insued, in which Frank Had Compleatley the Advantage, but the Wardmaster coming in put an end to the affray by knocking down the Cook, who was then marched to the Guardhouse & with him a number of the patients who had been Seen to laugh at the Sufferer.

As Soon as the Dr. heard what had happened, he ordered all the prisoners to be Liberated & Came to the hospital [where] he caught the Asst. in the act of beating one of the patients. He ordered him to Go to his room & to Consider himself a prisoner. He [Cathcart] Said he would See whether he was to be Confined for doing his duty. 'Go & when you are Sober I will talk to you.' 'I am as Sober as you are, Sir.' The Dr. now Called the Wardmaster & asked him if he thought Dr. Cathcart was Sober. He Said he did not know. 'Go, Call Wilson & Bryson here,' Said he [Salmon]. I had to Get up & Go into the Gallery where they were Standing. 'Look at that man,' Said Dr. Salmon; 'do you think him Sober or fit to have charge of 100 Sick men? I insist on your answer & you will have to Confirm what you Say now before a Court Martial.' I Said I did not Say absolutely Drunk, but I did not think that was he a proper Soldier the Adjutant would pass him for Guard. Wilson Swore point blank that he was 'as Drunk as ever I was in my life, & you know that it is not Long Since I was flogged for being drunk on parade'.

The next morning Dr. Salmon told Wilson & I not to take any medicine that Cathcart might order us, a Caution which was perfectly necessary as but a few Days after that there was a man brought to the hospital in the Brain fever who was in Such a Situation as required three people to hold him. Cathcart ordered him to be tied. Before they could Get this effected he broke one of the beds. The Dr. then went into the Surgery & brought out a Small glassful of Some thing which he gave him & in five minutes he fell asleep. But it proved a Sleep of Death, for he never awoke & Cathcart had him buried without [informing] Dr. Salmon that He was in the hospital. (N.B.: he was carried out a corpse in 6 Hours after being relieved off Guard.)

A few days after this the Dr. Said he was Going to Send me to Frontier, as he thought I would be much better there than in the Hospital & that he intended I Should remain there as long as the Regt. Remained on the Island, which I Suppose would have been the Case, but as Soon as Purss Deserted, the Adjutant,[69] who had the Command, Said that I would be the next & he did not blame me for it, but he was resolved I Should not Go from under his care. So he Sent me to the barrack.

However I was perfectly recovered and was Glad of Getting to Town, as I expected that my friend Corbet[70] would have found means to have Gone off, but in this I was mistaken, for as Soon as the Dr. Saw me he Sent me back again to Frontier. The Very next day there was a Corporal & 2 men ordered to be Sent to St. Mathew's Key, which lay at the End of St. Pierres about a mile from the Barracks & where the Capt[ain]s of Vessels Generally went for a walk on Sundays. And as I thought that this would be a Good Situation, I Spoke to the Serg[t.] who had Charge of us, & on treating him to a bottle of Rum he Recommended me to Go there & Said that as I never drank any, there would be no danger of my neglecting the Duty of the place, In consequence of this I was Sent for & asked if I would wish to Go there. I Said I would be Very happy to Go, if I was allowed to have another with me who I could rely on for behaving well. Well, said he, take anyone with you that you please. I named Sibbet[71] & he ordered him to Get ready. They took Care, however, to Send a Corporal with us that he knew would keep a sharp lookout upon us.

When we went there we found a Gunner of the Artillery there, under whose Command both the Corporal & us were. Sibbet & I resolved to ingratiate ourselves with him as much as possible, but we found him not at all disposed to befriend us &, what was worse, he would not drink any, So that we could not make him drunk, which we hoped might have been done & one of us would then have Gone to town to endeavour to make friends with Some Sailors, plenty of whom were disposed to befriend us had we had an oppurtunity of meeting them.

We had been a week on the battery without ever asking Liberty to Leave it, when one day we Saw 2 large Vessels preparing to Go out. We Consulted what would be the best means of Getting to town without Suspicion & at length resolved that Sibbet, of whom they had less Suspicion than me, Should, when we went to Gather wood, tear one of his Shoes & then he would have to Go to the Barracks to Get a new pair; & as I had a new pair, he would take them in his pocket & put them on as Soon as he Got to Town.

Before we went to the Battery I went to a plantation & purchased Some Sugar & Limes & as Soon as Sibbet went away I made a Jug of punch, in order to keep them from thinking the time long till he would Come back. Contrary to my expectation, before Sibbet came back I had them both Drunk & unfortunately an American Vessel attempted to Go out without Clearing out from the Custom house. In consequence of which, the fort on the Side of the Town next the Custom house fired at her, which was the Signal for our Battery to either force her back or Sink her. There was 7 32lb. Guns loaded, but none of them were in a direction to touch the Vessel & it was impossible for me to move any of them. However I resolved to light the Matches & fire the Guns & by the time I had Got my matches lighted, the Wind chopped round So that She had to Stand right by the Fort. As Soon as I found that the first Gun was Astern of her I fired it & immediately fired the next, which was then Considerably ahead of her. I then hailed her & told the Capt. to come on Shore. 'I am bound for Boston,' Said he & his men Gave a Cheer. I threw by the Trumpet & Seized the match again & Gave her a 3rd. Shot. The Capt. paid no attention to it. I hailed him again & his answer was Such as I Shall not Report. The Inst[ant] I heard it, I determined if possible that I would bring him back. With this intention I went to an old french Gun, which was better balanced than any of the Rest & with Considerable Difficulty Got it levelled & as Soon as I had brought it to bear I hailed him again, but Got no answer whatever. As Soon as I found that my french Gun would bear, I fired & Carried away part of her Q[uarterdeck] railing, which Soon made the Yankee Cease his Cavaliers & Hoist out his Boat. When he came to the fort he had to pay 120 Dollars for the 4 Shots & then Go & Clear out his Vessel at the Custom house. When Sibbet heard the Guns he came off as fast as possible & We Got a Good laugh at the Capt. when he came ashore. We proposed to him to take us off, which would prevent him from having his Vessel to clear acc[t]., as the other fort would not mind him after Seeing him ashore with us, but he would not consent & although we had all the inclination in the world to let him Go, yet we dared not do it.

Ab[ou]t Eight OClock the Gunner & Corporal Got better and on being told what had happened, the Gunner was frighted almost to Death Least we Should tell on him. But we found that after this he had less Suspicion of us than before.

One Evening that I was Down in Town I heard that two Ships that had Just discharged their Cargoes of Stores & were bound for Liverpool were to Go out that night. In consequence of this we Got a Jug of punch made & Sat down in the [hut] in which we lived to Drink it. One of the Vessels lay directly under the battery & as Soon as we heard her Boat called, Sibbet made Some excuse & ran down to the Boat, where he met the Lieut., who on Seeing him half Naked asked him what was wrong. He told him, nothing, but that him & his Comrade wished to Go to England with him, in case he wanted any hands. The Lieut. Said that he did want hands, but he Dared not take him as he Saw from the Cut of his hair that he was a Soldier. But, Said he, if you will come down when you hear our Bell Strike 10 Dressed in Sailor's Cloathes, I will take you on Board. Sibbet went Directly to town & Got 2 Sailors Jackets & as we had loose Trousers we were Compleated and were in the Greatest hopes that our troubles were at an end. But you may Guess what we felt on Seeing the Vessel [sail] out at 7 OClock.

After this, we never were So Sanguine in our expectations. Yet in the Course of a month our hopes of Liberty had been So often raised and Depressed that it had a considerable effect on our health. Sibbet in Particular Grew So bad that I expected he would Soon have to take to the Hospital, which would at once have put an end to all hopes of making an attempt at Escaping. We now Spent all our Money in buying milk & Flour, as that was the only thing that either of us could eat with Safety or Satisfaction & in a little time Sibbet Got better, & I worse. However we resolved at all events not to Go to the Hospital if we could possibly avoid it & to prevent this we used every means in our power to Ingratiate ourselves more into the Good Graces of the Corporal & Gunner. The latter being fond of Basil Tea, we Got a Little of it & then Set out to Look for more & the Second Day we went out we met with a Bed of it, which would have Served the whole Reg^t. for a month. From this we brought a large bundle & tied it to the branch of a tree to dry & we could Go every morning & Get us as much as would make our breakfast.

Neither Sibbet or I, however, dared to taste it, although we were both fond of it, as it is not allowed to be Good for people in the Situation that we were then in. This tea is an Herb that Grows Spontaneously in old Ground in most parts of the Island & is thought by most people to be Superior to Chinese Tea. But it is not allowed to be taken to England & half a lb. of it will condemn both Vessel & Cargo in that Land of Liberty. This is one of the many evils that arises to England by the Government Giving Individuals an Exclusive Right to the trade or Commerce of any Spot or part of her Dominions.

Before Sibbet was recovered properly, I was So much worse that I was Scarce able to be out of my Hammock, but Still persisted in my Determination of not Going to the Hospital. But one day the Dr. took it into his head to come & Visit the battery and as it was contrary to Regulations to bring his horse on the Platform, he called me to Go & hold him till he would take a walk round it. I was worse that Morning than I had been for Some time & as Soon as I Got up the Light forsook my Eyes & I fell Down. The Dr. Got hold of me, else I Should have fallen over the bank & in all probability ended my life. When I recovered, the Dr. was threatening the Corporal with everything that it was in his power to hurt him in, for not Sending me to the Hospital, & as Soon as I was able to look about me he told me he would Soon find a way to punish me. I told him it was very hard that a man Should be punished for Going to the Hospital when he was not well & for not Going I did not find myself worse. 'I intended to Soon Come to you, either this Evening or tomorrow.' 'Well,' Said he, 'I would be inclined to believe you had I not Seen you a few days back & then you looked much improved & now you are as thin and Death like as my Whip. Bring my horse here, Sibbet.' As Soon as the horse was brought he ordered me to be put on his back & the Corporal to take me to the Hospital. In vain I pleaded to be left there 2 days longer. He would not hear a word. 'Well then,' Said I, 'you may as well kill me at once as Send me to the

Hospital.' 'Well then, you must Sit there,' Said he, 'for I am resolved not to Draw any blame on myself by humouring you.'

The Dr. walked all the way to the Hospital with us & as Soon as we Got there Gave orders that I Should have neither wine nor any Extra provision Served to me. 'I will Soon make you repent Staying from this [place] till you are Dead & then Coming to me to Get buried.' I threw myself on a bed, more cast down than I had ever been in my life. I was Sorry that I had offended the Dr. & mad at being taken from the only place on the Island from whence there was any probability of organising my Escape from. I Loathed the Hospital & Everything I Saw. At length, the ward Master began to Serve out the wine, the Smell of which turned my heart & I went out & Vomited to Such a Degree that the Serg$^{t.}$ Sent for the Dr. who, when he came, ordered me an Emetic & then to be put to bed & to Get nothing but Barley Water till the next morning. When he came in the Morning he ordered me a pint of Milk & 2 Eggs & to have 3 Glasses of wine at 12 OClock, which was one more than the allowance. About 10 OClock Sibbet brought my Hammock to me & that was the last time I Saw him till I met him in Philadelphia, as he Got off in 3 days after.

This Circumstance you may be Sure was not much in my favour. Indeed, for 10 days I Scarce knew what was doing about me & I Suppose I Should have Died So, had the Dr. not Sent me once more to Frontier where, contrary to my Expectation, the Adj$^{t.}$ rec[eive]d me with as much kindness as Ever & Even Said that he believed I was Ignorant of Sibbet's Going off. He Gave me Liberty to walk about as much as I pleased in the Mornings & Evenings, & to this I believe I was in Some measure Indebted for my recovery.

The Dr. had ordered me to be kept in Frontier till the Reg$^{t.}$ would be ordered off the Island & as Soon as I Got pretty well recovered the Adj$^{t.}$ ordered me to Go to Town & Get the men's provisions for them. This was the Very thing I wished for, as it Gave me an oppurtunity of Going to & Through any part of the Town I pleased & I was Still in hopes that my friend Corbet would be able to assist me in Getting off.

I had not been long at there till I was ordered to my Duty, in consequence of 2 men making their Escape when in Town on pass. I was not yet master of my Exercise, So had very hard Duty to perform, but my health being Good, I kept up my Spirits with the thought that Some procurable oppurtunity would offer & that I might be the better able to Embrace it Should it occur. I laboured hard to keep both my person & arms as Clean as possible, which So far Gained me the Goodwill of the officers that I could Get a pass to Town when no other person who had to attend Drill Dared to ask it.

I Still depended on Corbet, but I Soon Found that I was Depending on a broken Reed, as he would not Do any thing unless it would turn out for his own private Interest. I took care, however, not to break with him, as he had me compleatly in his power & I had Still Some faint hopes that an oppurtunity would offer that might put Something in his pocket & Give me Liberty at the Same time.

I believe I have already informed you since my arrival in America of the Principal occurances that happened to me after this, So [I] Shall not report them now as I am perfectly sick of the business & I am well Convinced that you are more So. I am inclined to Send it off by a Vessel that sails tomorrow for Belfast. As I Should have made Some Comments on what you have now Read & likewise endeavoured to have Given you Some Idea of the Situation of the Poor Negroes, however, the former you are able to do better than I & the Latter David[72] has Given you a tolerable Idea of. I have only to Request that you will write me your Sentiments on my Conduct which I have faithfully laid before you & in Excuse for the many Errors in principal & practice I can only Say that I hope with the Disagreeable Situation I was placed in often put it out of my power to act agreeably to my own inclination. I feel myself however perfectly Justifiable in Saying that I have never in any Instance Deviated from that Rectitude of Conduct which Should be the Characteristick both of a man & a Christian. Except when drove to it by fatal Necessity & however I may be blamed by those who can only Judge by the seeing of the Eyes, I hope that I Shall be admitted by him who Judges the Heart.

I Do not Expect you will be able to Read the one half of it. I know I am none of the best Scribes at any time, but in this I have Seldom wrote more than half a Dozen Lines at once & then in the greatest haste. I intended not to have Sent it till the fall & to have [revised?] it in the autumn, but as there is a Conveyance now I thought it better to Send it and let you Correct it for your Self, & then you will be the better pleased with it. And Even if I had kept it, it is probable that I might not have Got time to do it better then than it is now, as I thought when I began that I Should have little else to Do all winter, but in Consequence of the Peace, Business got So Dull that almost ¼ of the Merch^{ts.} of this City have failed & in consequence of this, instead of Sitting at the Desk, I had to Run about all weathers looking for Money, which has been So Scarce all the winter that People who would have paid their Bills without ever looking at them before, were no longer Looking at them at all now. It is Estimated that the amount of the Different Failures in the Last 4 months is 12 Million of Dollars among which The People I live with have lost about 12 Thousand. About a week ago I Set out to the Country looking for Some [debts] & Intended to have Stayed away a week had I Saw any likelihood of Getting any, but finding that I was not Likely to Get as much as would pay horse hire I Returned the Same evening, after being about 30 miles out, & was Just Ten Dollars poorer when I returned than when I went away. Whereupon I put an end to my Country *Jaunt*.

I must beg you to excuse me to the host of my Friends to whom I Should have wrote at this time, as I do not Expect to be able to Get this finished before 12 Oclock at Night & The Vessel Cleared out & to Sail with the morning Tide. I must also beg your particular attention to what I Said before Respecting this long Letter, Viz. Not to Expose the writer by letting any person See it Through Mottives of Curiousity, as It was not wrote to Gratify any Such person, but to Shew you how Great things God Has done for me in first preserving my life amids Sour according Death, & Afterwards in his own Good time & by the means which he thought best, Delivering me from the hands of mine Enemies. For which & for all his other mercies I know you will Redily Join with me in ascribing to a three [in] One God all praise, honour & Glory, world without End, Amen.

I am happy to have it in my power to inform you of the welfare of your friends in this Country so far as I am Acquainted. We have had no letters from Edward Stone Since our friend Mr. Queen left, which is Something Singular, but I Suppose that on acc[t.] of the fineness of the winter they have found more pleasure in Jaunting about than in writing to us. David had a Letter from Robert Millekan yesterday. All our friends in Philadelphia are well & Mrs. Purss is or is about to present John with an addition to his family.[73] But the Greatest News is the Marriage of Sally McCormick to Dan Davidson. This piece of Intelligence we Rec[eive]d by a Letter from Wm. Finlay to A. Queen who had Rec[eive]d the acc[t.] from young Mr. Cummings of Ballimore So I believe you may Depend on it as fact.

We have lately had another melancholy instance of the Effects of a *Dissolute* youth in our friend James Finlay who for some time had been in the Same State as Dr. Barr was in my Uncle Samuel's, with this difference that he was in a great Degree deprived of his Senses. At present he is Quite well.

We have had a most Remarkable open Winter here & acc[ts.] from Europe say that you had a most Severe one with you. I hope, however, that you have not felt much of it. You may tell John Queen if he is Still an inhabitant of Ballyalton that he has incurred the Displeasure of all his friends in America by not Writing as he promised by Liverpool as Soon as he arrived. Please also Inform him that the Congress of the United States has reduced the Period of Residence before becoming a Citizen of the United States to 5 Years, & it is Expected the Senate will Make it *3 years*. The Republicans have Carried every thing before them.[74]

Please Give my Compliments to my Mother, Sisters & Brother, & to all Friends in Ballyallaugh, Ballyrat & Cotton etc. etc. If Dr. Dickson is among the Number of Prisoners who have been Liberated,[75] please call on him & present my Compliments on the occation, Likewise to Mrs. & Miss Dickson and assure them that in Common with the Rest of their Republican Friends in [New] York I Sincerely rejoice at their Situation. I would be Glad to hear of the rest of the Fort George & barrack room Prisoners, Particularly Messrs. Teeling, McGinnis & Falloon.[76] If you

See the Dr. he will be able to inform you of all, or if he is Still a prisoner please ask Mrs. or Miss Dickson. You can Scarce imagine the Interest I take in their Concerns & I am Sorry to Say that Lexon, whome I asked to Call on Mrs. Dickson, has not Executed my Commission in a Very Satisfactory manner. For which I mean to Give him a Good Dressing as Soon as I can Get time. This Intimation will, I hope, forwarn you in your Communications on this Subject.

Your Affectionate Brother
And^{w.} Bryson

Abbreviations

DNB	*Dictionary of National Biography*
HO	Home Office
KCRO	Kent County Record Office, Maidstone
NAI	National Archives, Dublin
NAM	National Army Museum, London
PRO	Public Record Office, London
PRONI	Public Record Office of Northern Ireland
Reb. Pap.	Rebellion Papers (NAI)
Rep. Sec. Com. (Commons)	*Report of the Secret Committee of the [Irish] House of Commons* (Dublin, 1798)
Rep. Sec. Com. (Lords)	*Report of the Secret Committee of the [Irish] House of Lords* (Dublin, 1798)

Notes to Introduction

1   Shakespeare, *Henry IV, Part 2*, III, i.

2   Family details have been taken from the Robb Papers in PRONI, T1454/2,3. Andrew Bryson was described as a tanner in *Dublin Evening Post*, 15 Sept. 1798.

3   See below, p. 10, and *DNB* for James and William Bryson.

4   For the Volunteers see R. B. McDowell, 'Colonial Nationalism and the Winning of Parliamentary Independence' in T. W. Moody and W. E. Vaughan (eds), *A New History of Ireland*, iv: *Eighteenth-Century Ireland, 1691–1800* (Oxford, 1986), pp. 196–216; R. B. McDowell, *Ireland in the Age of Imperialism and Revolution, 1760–1801* (Oxford, 1979), ch. 5; A. T. Q. Stewart, *A Deeper Silence: The Hidden Origins of the United Irishmen* (London, 1993); P. D. H. Smyth, 'The Volunteers and Parliament, 1779–84' in Thomas Bartlett and D. W. Hayton (eds), *Penal Era and Golden Age: Essays in Irish History* (Belfast, 1979), pp. 113–36.

5   Probably the best discussion of Presbyterianism can be found in Peter Brooke, *Ulster Presbyterianism: The Historical Perspective, 1610–1970* (Dublin, 1987).

6   Charles Hamilton Teeling, *Sequel to the History of the Irish Rebellion of 1798: A Personal Narrative* (Glasgow, n.d. [1828?]), p. 186; [John Binns], *Recollections of the Life of John Binns: Twenty-Nine Years in Europe and Fifty-Three in the United States* (Philadelphia, 1854), pp. 52–3.

7   William Steel Dickson, *Scripture Politics* (Belfast, 1812; repr., ed. Brendan Clifford, Belfast, 1991), p. 20. Some sources, e.g, Charles Dickson, *Revolt in the North: Antrim and Down in 1798* (Dublin, 1960), p. 83, suggest that £60,000 was spent by the Londonderry family on this election, but H. Montgomery Hyde, *The Rise of Castlereagh* (London, 1933) offers the more reasonable sum of £6,000.

8 T. A. Emmet, Arthur O'Connor and W. J. MacNeven, 'Memoir' in William J. MacNeven (ed.), *Pieces of Irish History* (New York, 1807), p. 29.

9 Samuel McSkimin [*sic*], *Annals of Ulster* (new ed., Belfast, 1906), p. 5.

10 Nancy J. Curtin, *The United Irishmen: Popular Politics in Ulster and Dublin, 1791–1798* (Oxford, 1994), p. 92.

11 The Defenders was an oath-bound secret society which had emerged in Co. Armagh in the 1780s to protect Catholics from the depredations of Protestant groups such as the Peep o' Day Boys. By 1792–93 it had spread into Counties Down, Louth, Cavan and Meath. Its aims were a mixture: the redress of local grievances, a 'Jacobin' programme of anticlericalism and support for revolutionary France, and an inchoate and millenarian desire for the restoration of Gaelic culture and the promotion of Catholic revanchism. By 1796 the revolutionary United Irish movement had absorbed the Defenders, much to the confusion of the authorities. See Camden to Portland, 6 Aug. 1796: PRO, HO 100/62, ff. 154–6; Emmet, 'Memoir', pp. 140–44; Thomas Bartlett, 'Defenders and Defenderism in 1795', *Irish Historical Studies,* xxiv (1984–85), pp. 373–94; Tom Garvin, 'Defenders, Ribbonmen and Others: Underground Political Networks in Pre-Famine Ireland' in C. H. E. Philpin (ed.), *Nationalism and Popular Protest in Ireland* (Cambridge, 1987), pp. 219–44; Marianne Elliott, 'The Defenders in Ulster' in David Dickson, Dáire Keogh and Kevin Whelan (eds), *The United Irishmen: Republicanism, Radicalism and Rebellion* (Dublin 1993), pp. 222–33.

12 McDowell, *Ireland in the Age of Imperialism*, pp. 351–461; Curtin, *United Irishmen,* pp. 38–66.

13 Emmet *et al.*, 'Memoir', p. 211; Charles Hamilton Teeling, *The History of the Irish Rebellion of 1798: A Personal Narrative* (Glasgow, 1828), pp. 5, 9–10.

14 *Rep. Sec. Com. (Lords),* pp. 7–8; Curtin, *United Irishmen,* pp. 102–3.

15 Thomas Graham, ' "An Union of Power"? The United Irish Organisation, 1795–1798' in Dickson *et al.* (eds), *United Irishmen,* pp. 246–7.

16 Edmond A. McNaughton to Arthur Wolfe, 9 May 1795: KCRO, U840/0146/8.

17 For a long list of the different tactics used by United Irish emissaries see KCRO, U840/0151/1. See also deposition of Robert Carlisle, 2 Apr. 1796: Reb. Pap., 620/23/65.

18 'J. H. Smith' to Edward Cooke, 23 July 1796: PRO, HO 100/62, f. 142; Cooke to General Nugent, 25 July 1796: NAM, Nugent Papers, 6807/174, ff. 147–8; 'J.W.' [Leonard McNally] to Cooke, 5 Oct. 1796: Reb. Pap., 620/10/121/38.

19 — to Cooke, 27 Nov. 1796: ibid., 620/26/83; Col. James Durham to Rev. Clotworthy Soden, 29 May 1796: ibid., 620/23/129; James Waddell to [Cooke], 1 July 1796: ibid., 620/24/1; Sir George Hill to Pelham, 20 Mar. 1797: ibid., 620/29/96.

20 *Rep. Sec. Com. (Commons),* pp. 6, 14–15, 63; Dickson, *Revolt in the North,* p. 116;

McSkimin, *Annals of Ulster*, p. 50; Cooke to Nugent, n.d. [1796]: NAM, Nugent Papers, 6807/174, ff. 149–50.

21   Pelham to Lake, 3 Mar. 1797: NAM, Nugent Papers, 6807/174, ff. 222–9.

22   Durham to Soden, 29 May 1796: Reb. Pap., 620/23/129; Andrew MacNeven to Pelham, 24 Feb. 1796: ibid., 620/23/36.

23   *Rep. Sec. Com. (Commons)*, p. 58; Curtin, *United Irishmen*, p. 113.

24   I presume that it was Andrew senior and not Andrew junior who was arrested, for his occupation was given as farmer. See McDowell, *Ireland in the Age of Imperialism*, p. 574.

25   [Dublin] *The Press*, 21, 25 Nov. 1797.

26   James Smyth, 'Dublin's Political Undergound in the 1790s' in Gerard O'Brien (ed.), *Parliament, Politics and People: Essays in Eighteenth-Century Irish History* (Dublin, 1989), p. 144.

27   *Rep. Sec. Com. (Commons)*, p. 3; Dickson, *Revolt in the North*, p. 114.

28   *Rep. Sec. Com. (Commons)*, pp. 144–53; William Fox, 'Narrative of the Proceedings of the Rebel Army in the County Down': Reb. Pap., 620/4/41; John Caldwell, 'Particulars of History of a North County Irish Family': PRONI, T3541/53/3, pp. 70, 107. Inexplicably, A. T. Q. Stewart in his *The Summer Soldiers: The 1798 Rebellion in Antrim and Down* (Belfast, 1995) attributes Fox's narrative to another Down licentiate, David Bailie Warden.

29   Black Book of Northern Ireland: PRONI, D272/1. A list of rebel officers, based on information from Lisburn, dated 18 July 1798, which gives Bryson's rank as captain, was based on outdated information: PRONI, D162/98; *Rep. Sec. Com. (Commons)*, p. 156.

30   Magin's report: PRO, HO 100/77, ff. 44–6.

31   *Rep. Sec. Com. (Commons)*, p. 160.

32   Magin's report: PRO, HO 100/77, ff. 44–6.

33   Thomas D'Arcy McGee, *A History of the Irish Settlers in North America* (Boston, 1851), p. 83.

34   Fox's narrative: Reb. Pap., 620/4/61.

35   See below, p. 76.

36   Londonderry to Castlereagh, n.d. [late Mar. 1799]: Reb. Pap., 620/8/85/13.

37   Nugent to Castlereagh, 26 July 1798: ibid., 620/3/32/11.

38   His name was spelt Brison in the published list: *Dublin Evening Post*, 15 Sept. 1798. Bryson's name was placed on the Fugitive Act by Under-Secretary Edward Cooke. Cooke to Nugent, 12 Aug. 1798: PRONI, 272/40.

39   Cooke to Nugent, 12 Aug. 1798: PRONI, 272/40. 'List of Officers Serving in the Rebel Army', 18 July 1798: PRONI, D162/98.

40   [Littlehales?] to Nugent, 29 Sept. 1798: PRO, HO 100/86, f. 70.

41   *Memoirs and Correspondence of Viscount Castlereagh, Second Marquess of Londonderry,*

ed. Charles Vane, Marquess of Londonderry (12 vols, London, 1848–54), i, 149–50.

42 Of the 405 rebels sentenced to death by court martial, 273 (32.5 per cent) had their sentences commuted to a lesser punishment (normally to banishment or to general service overseas). It is possible that Cornwallis did not personally review many of the sentences passed in June and early July 1798, so his leniency may be underestimated by these figures. The data come from my own research towards a study of the fate of Irish rebel prisoners in the period 1797 to 1804.

43 For examples of interest being successfully exerted see Castlereagh to William Wickham, 6 Feb. 1799: PRO, HO 100/88, ff. 88–90; Reb. Pap., 620/3/19/7; 620/3/23/1; 620/3/28/6, 7, 18.

44 Cornwallis to Portland, 29 Oct. 1798: *Correspondence of Charles, First Marquis Cornwallis*, ed. Charles Ross (3 vols, London, 1859), ii, 428.

45 See below, p. 22.

46 New Geneva was being fitted up for the reception of prisoners in August 1798. See *Dublin Evening Post*, 23 Aug. 1798.

47 Marianne Elliott, *Wolfe Tone: Prophet of Irish Independence* (New Haven, 1989), p. 398.

48 Cooke to Wickham, 12 Nov. 1798: *Cornwallis Correspondence*, ii, 435. For Castlereagh's views see Castlereagh to William Wickham, 16 Nov. 1798: *Castlereagh Correspondence*, i, 445–7.

49 The first orders went out to regional commanders in November. H. Taylor to Major-General French, 21 Nov. 1798: PRO, HO 100/86, f. 44. The order to Belfast followed a month later. [Cooke?] to Brigadier-General Campbell, 23 Dec. 1798: PRO, HO100/86, f. 100.

50 Castlereagh to John King, 31 Jan. 1799: PRO, HO 100/88, f. 82.

51 For a fuller examination of Bryson's account in context see Michael Durey, 'Crossing the Line in 1799: Plebeian Moral Economy on the High Seas', *Mariner's Mirror,* lxxx (1994), pp. 209–14.

52 Sir Richard Levinge, *Historical Records of the Forty-Third Regiment, Monmouthshire Light Infantry* (London, 1868), p. 93. The 43rd was not a light infantry regiment in Bryson's time. It was reorganised in England in 1803 and thereafter played a major role in Robert Craufurd's Light Division during the Peninsular War.

53 For a very full account see Michael Duffy, *Soldiers, Sugar and Seapower: The British Expeditions to the West Indies and the War against Revolutionary France* (Oxford, 1987), esp. ch. 14. See also [Jonathan Leach], *Rough Sketches of the Life of an Old Soldier, during a service in the West Indies* . . . (Cambridge, 1831; repr., Cambridge, 1986), pp. 10–19.

54 Samuel Bryson to Samuel Finlay, 10 Mar. 1799: PRONI, T1454/2/3.

55 Bryson refers to a new Naturalisation Act reducing the period of domicile in America to five years. This act was passed by Congress in 1804.

56   Duffy, *Soldiers, Sugar and Seapower*, pp. 329–30.

57   Alexander Marsden to Castlereagh, 10 Oct. 1799: *Castlereagh Correspondence*, ii, 417.

58   It is possible that Bryson's sister Elizabeth was also in America. See Nelly Robb to David Bryson, 22 Mar. 1806: PRONI, T1454/2/3.

59   Caldwell, 'North County Family', pp. 119–20; Nugent to Alexander Marsden, 27 Mar. 1799: Reb. Pap., 620/8/85/13.

60   Andrew Bryson Sr gave his occupation as grocer when he sought naturalisation in 1802. Kenneth Scott, *Early New York Naturalizations* (Baltimore, 1981), p. 206. I am grateful to Miriam Touba of the New-York Historical Society for giving me this reference.

61   The latest account of Irish exiles in America at this time is Michael Durey, *Transatlantic Radicals and the Early American Republic* (Lawrence, Kans., 1997).

62   Nelly Robb to Andrew Bryson Sr, 22 Mar. 1805: PRONI, T1454/3/1; Nelly Robb to David Bryson, 22 Mar. 1806: ibid., T1454/2/3.

63   Isabella Bryson's petition to Duke of Richmond, n.d. [1807?]: ibid., T1454/3/4.

64   David Bryson was active in the New York Hibernian Provident Society. See [Philadelphia] *Aurora*, 16 Oct. 1807.

65   Robb–Bryson–Finlay family tree: PRONI, T1454/2/1; *Appleton's Cyclopaedia of American Biography* (12 vols, New York, 1876–87), i, 428.

66   Durey, *Transatlantic Radicals*, p. 212.

Notes to Narrative

1   The prison tender was the *Postlethwaite*.

2   Many of the prisoners were hoping that their sentences would be reduced, relying on the favourable influence on government of friends and neighbours.

3   John Dickey, shopkeeper, of Crumlin, Co. Antrim. Found guilty of treason and rebellion in July 1798 at a court martial in Lisburn and sentenced to transportation. There seems to have been some doubt about the sentence, for in August 1798 he was offered, but refused, the opportunity to sign General Nugent's proclamation which would have enabled him to expatriate himself. NAI, Reb. Pap., 620/39/203. He was probably the brother of James Dickey, a Crumlin attorney, who was executed for his role in the rebellion.

4   Luke Teeling, a prominent Catholic linen draper from Lisburn, had been involved in politics since being a delegate from Antrim to the Catholic Convention which met in Dublin in December 1792. Throughout the 1790s he was the acknowledged Catholic leader in Ulster. He remained on the tender until about October

1799, when he was transferred to Carrickfergus Castle. He was not released until at least 1803, after an imprisonment of more than five years, during which time he consistently refused to accept any form of oath of allegiance offered by the government. PRONI, 272/14; Charles Hamilton Teeling, *Sequel to the History of the Irish Rebellion of 1798: A Personal Narrative* (Belfast, 1832; repr., Glasgow, 1876), pp. 322–35.

5   William Steel Dickson (1744–1824) was the New Light Presbyterian minister at Portaferry. A vigorous supporter of the American patriots in their war of independence and an active Volunteer, in the early 1790s Dickson was one of the most outspoken radicals in Ulster. In 1798 he was made commander -in-chief of the Down United Irishmen, but was arrested on 5 June just before the insurrection. He was never brought to trial. In March 1799 he was transferred with nineteen other Belfast and Dublin state prisoners to Fort George in Scotland. He was released in 1802. His own account of this period can be found in *A Narrative of the Confinement and Exile of William Steel Dickson* (Dublin, 1812), much of which has been reprinted, with commentary, in *Scripture Politics*, ed. Brendan Clifford (Belfast, 1991).

6   The tender was far less crowded than it had been in the summer. There were 36 on board when Teeling's party of 24 arrived, but 12 left with Bryson the next day.

7   This is probably a reference to Rev. William Bryson (1730–1815), Presbyterian minister at Antrim, who was a staunch loyalist in 1798. See *DNB* entry.

8   26 December 1798.

9   William Stavely, Covenanting (i.e. Reformed Presbyterian) minister of Conlig, near Newtownards, and captain of the Drumbracken Volunteers. A millenarian, he was one of three Covenanting clergymen who stirred up passions at large open-air meetings in Ulster in 1796 and 1797. He denied being a United Irishman, but probably was a senior officer. He was imprisoned for a month in 1797 and arrested again in June 1798. Always complaining when on the prison ship, he was never tried and eventually was released and became minister at Cullybackey. *Northern Star*, 22 Dec. 1792; Peter Brooke, 'Controversies in Ulster Presbyterianism, 1790–1836' (Ph.D. thesis, Cambridge University, 1980), pp. 29–33; John Caldwell, 'Particulars of the History of a North County Irish Family': PRONI, T3541/5/3, p. 117. (Caldwell was a United Irishman exiled to America in 1798.)

10   Probably a kinsman of Luke Teeling. The United Irishman John Fitzsimons was Teeling's son-in-law.

11   Bernard McGinnis [Magenis], Catholic priest from Calra, Co. Down. A colonel in the military wing of the United Irishmen and member of the Down county committee. He refused Nugent's proclamation in August 1798 and was still in prison in July 1799. PRONI, D272/1, 14; Reb. Pap., 620/39/203.

12   Possibly Cleland Colvin, a carpenter from Newtownards, who in June 1798 was
      sentenced to 800 lashes for seditious practices, of which he received 600. *Dublin
      Evening Post*, 12 June 1798.

13   Margaret Munro, *née* Johnston, was the wife of Henry Munro, the Lisburn linen
      merchant who replaced Dickson as commander of the Down forces. He fought
      at the battle of Ballynahinch and was executed on 16 June 1798. Charles Dick-
      son, *Revolt in the North: Antrim and Down in 1798* (Dublin, 1960), pp. 199–201.

14   Colonel William Lumley of the 22nd Dragoons. He was wounded leading a reck-
      less cavalry charge along the main street at the battle of Antrim. He later became
      a distinguished cavalry general. Samuel McSkimin [*sic*], *Annals of Ulster* (new ed.,
      Belfast, 1906), p. 79; R. B. McDowell, *Ireland in the Age of Imperialism and Revolu-
      tion* (Oxford, 1979), p. 637.

15   Hillsborough was the seat of the Hill family, whose head, Arthur, 2nd Marquess
      of Downshire, was a leading loyalist who raised his own yeomanry force from
      among his tenants in 1797.

16   Now Jonesborough.

17   Now Ravensdale Park.

18   The jailer was Denis Fitzpatrick.

19   'Croppy' was a term of abuse used by loyalists of the radicals, being coined about
      1791 when sympathisers with the French Revolution cropped their hair in the
      revolutionary fashion.

20   Rev. Andrew Bryson, a noted linguist and antiquarian, was involved in the Gaelic
      revival at this time. Mary McNeill, *The Life and Times of Mary Ann McCracken,
      1770–1866* (Belfast, 1988), p. 79.

21   The jailer was John Allen.

22   Bartholomew Teeling, eldest son of Luke, was a leading United Irishman who
      spent time in France helping with invasion plans. He was captured with Hum-
      bert's forces at Ballinamuck, court-martialled in Dublin, and executed on 24 Sep-
      tember 1798. *Dublin Evening Post*, 20, 25 Sept. 1798.

23   A shillelagh, a stout cudgel.

24   The Marshalsea was the debtors' prison in Dublin.

25   The place-name was omitted, but was possibly either Clondalkin or Rathcoole.

26   The rebels alluded to were groups of bandits holding out in the Wicklow moun-
      tains following the rebellion. The most famous gang was led by Michael Dwyer.

27   Gawin Watts was one of two fugitives captured with Henry Joy McCracken, the
      United Irish commander in Antrim. Tried at Carrickfergus in August 1798, he
      was sentenced to seven years' transportation, which was later reduced to exile in
      America. McSkimin, *Annals*, p. 89.

28   Probably Samuel Adams of Killynure, who was on the Down county committee
      in November 1797. PRONI, D272/1.

29 Sentence unfinished in the manuscript.

30 The Naas jailer was James Dalton.

31 Bryson was probably not exaggerating the youthfulness of the officer; thirteen-year-olds were on active service in regiments in Ireland at this time. See, for example, Owen Dudley Edwards, *Burke and Hare* (Edinburgh, 1980), p. 16.

32 I.e. New Geneva, the holding camp near Waterford.

33 For more on *habeas corpus* at this time see Introduction, p. 11.

34 I.e. to commandeer.

35 Leighlinbridge.

36 Possibly Eldred Pottinger of Mount Pottinger, who in May 1797 acted as secretary at the unofficial freeholders' meeting held in Ballynahinch to protest against the imposition of the Insurrection Act and the activities of the army in Co. Down. Arrested soon after, his fields were among many harvested by large groups of United Irish sympathisers expressing their solidarity with those imprisoned without trial. Camden to Portland, 1 Nov. 1796: PRO, HO 100/62, ff. 314–18 (for the widespread nature of this form of harvesting in the north); McSkimin, *Annals*, p. 47; Jonathan Bardon, *A History of Ulster* (Belfast, 1992), p. 230.

37 Evidently, Knocktopher Castle, demolished by Cromwell in 1649. According to Samuel Lewis, 'there are no remains of the castle, but the mount and the fosse are still entire'. See *A Topographical Dictionary of Ireland* (2 vols, London, 1837), ii, 241.

38 John McKnight was found guilty of treason and rebellion at a Newtownards court martial in August 1798, being sentenced to general service overseas for life. Reb. Pap., 620/3/28/13. I have been unable to discover anything about Stone.

39 John Boyd of Ravarra, a member of the Down county committee in February 1798. PRONI, D272/1.

40 John Purse, sentenced for treason and rebellion at a court martial at Newtownards in July 1798 to general service for life. Reb. Pap., 620/3/28/13.

41 Bryson's attempt at *chevaux-de-frise*, a form of defensive outwork consisting of iron spikes set in palings, as used by seventeenth-century Frisians to repel cavalry.

42 The 'Jaegers' were Hessians, the 5th Battalion, 60th Regiment of Foot, commanded by Lieut.-Col. de Rottenburg. Three hundred strong, they acted as the guard for the prisoners on the voyage to Martinique. Cornwallis to Portland, 15 Mar. 1799, PRO, HO 100/83.

43 This curious denomination may represent a quarter-moidore, a Portuguese coin circulating in Bangor, Co. Down, in the early eighteenth century, when it was valued at 7s sterling (exchangeable for 7s 7d in Irish currency). See John Stevenson, *Two Centuries of Life in Down, 1600–1800* (revised ed., Belfast, 1990), p. 265.

44 Passage is the name of the embarkation point at Waterford.

45 Duncannon Fort.

46   The ship they were to travel on was the *Admiral de Vries*, a sixty-eight-gun third-rate man-of-war captured from the Dutch in 1797. In 1799 it was in the Transport Service, stationed at Portsmouth. Once in the West Indies, it was used as a prison ship in Jamaica.

47   According to *Steel's Royal Navy List*, the captain's name was J. Wright.

48   Bryson obviously was not aware of the role of the master on a ship.

49   *Steel's Navy List* fails to give a name to the ship's purser.

50   The regulation space (breadth) for hammocks on Royal Navy ships at this time was fourteen inches. Christopher Lloyd, *The British Seaman* (London, 1970), p. 224.

51   Burgoo, a form of porridge.

52   Moss, in Scots and evidently Ulster-Scots dialect, signifies bog or turf.

53   Knees are right-angled wooden or metal bars which provide strengthening and support at points of intersection of timbers in a ship.

54   In the eighteenth century 'the line' was the Tropic of Cancer, not the Equator.

55   The women of the Hessian troops seem not to have been treated by Mrs Neptune. The Hessian regiment had 23 women and 9 children with them. PRO, HO 100/83.

56   It is impossible to identify this particular Byrne, but he may have been one of three of this surname, Martin, Mathew and Patrick, sentenced to general service overseas by a court martial in Slane in July 1798.

57   John Greer, of Co. Down, found guilty of exciting [*sic*] rebellion by a Belfast court martial in July 1798. He was sentenced to life transportation (to Botany Bay), but the penalty was reduced to general service overseas. Reb. Pap., 620/3/28/19.

58   William Patton was found guilty at a court martial in July 1798 of treason and rebellion, viz. forcing another to join the rebels at Cairgaver Hill on 10 June 1798. His defence was that he surrendered his arms on 11 June and went back to his business until arrested. He was sentenced to life transportation. *Dublin Evening Post*, 10 July 1798; *Freeman's Journal*, 14 July 1798.

59   The name of the officer is impossible to decipher, but it may possibly be Captain Edward Hull of the 43rd Regiment. For a list of the officers who survived the tour of duty in Martinique to return to Britain in 1800, see Sir Richard George Augustus Levinge, *Historical Records of the Forty-Third Regiment, Monmouthshire Light Infantry* (London, 1868), p. 94.

60   The grenadier company of each regiment usually was made up of the tallest, fittest and most competent soldiers, who became the (prestigious) flank company.

61   According to army records, the regimental doctor was Robert Salmon.

62   Toast-water: water in which toasted bread has been steeped, used as a drink for invalids, etc.

63   See preceding note.

64   Bryson later gives the assistant surgeon's name as Cathcart, who, however, is not listed as such in army records. According to the records, the position was held by Thomas Cooke in 1797, and by one Sullivan when the regiment returned to Britain in 1800. Evidently Cathcart's appointment was an unofficial one during the intervening period.

65   I have been unable to determine what Bryson meant by 'partis', unless it be an Ulster rendering of 'patties.' For 'toast' see note 62.

66   Captain John Cameron, who was still in the regiment when it was part of the Light Brigade in the Peninsula a decade later.

67   The 'hopeful recruits of 1796' were probably Defenders from Connacht whom Lord Carhampton forced into the armed forces when he purged the region in 1795.

68   Possibly a snack.

69   Lieut. R. Kipling (or Kippling) became adjutant in May 1799.

70   Probably a brother or cousin of Thomas and William Corbet, who were part of the Irish fugitive community in France after 1798.

71   John Sibbet of Killinchy in June 1798 was charged with taking two horses from the stables of a Mr Gordon with the intention of assisting the rebels, with housebreaking, and with carrying arms. He was found guilty of the last two charges. Because of his youth, his sentence was to serve in the army overseas for life. *Dublin Evening Post*, 3 July 1798. His father was named in the Fugitive Act.

72   Bryson's elder brother.

73   It cannot be confirmed that this was the John Purse who was with Bryson in the West Indies. Another John (*recte* Jonathan) Purse was also involved in the rebellion. On 23 June 1798 he was found guilty at a Maghera, Co. Londonderry, court martial of being a rebel officer in arms and was sentenced to life transportation. Reb. Pap., 620/3/19/2.

74   Congress altered the residency period for naturalisation from fourteen to five years in 1804.

75   Rev. William Steel Dickson was one of twenty rebel leaders imprisoned in Fort George, Scotland, from March 1799. Most of the Belfast prisoners among them were released on security and allowed back to Ireland early in 1801.

76   Luke Teeling was kept in prison in Carrickfergus until at least 1803. Father Bernard McGinnis and Francis Falloon were banished in 1799.

Bibliography

Bardon, Jonathan, *A History of Ulster* (Belfast, 1992)

Brooke, Peter, *Ulster Presbyterianism: The Historical Perspective, 1610–1970* (Dublin, 1987)

Curtin, Nancy, *The United Irishmen: Popular Politics in Ulster and Dublin, 1791–1798* (Oxford, 1994)

Dickson, Charles, *Revolt in the North: Antrim and Down in 1798* (Dublin, 1960)

Dickson, David, Keogh, Dáire, and Whelan, Kevin (eds), *The United Irishmen: Republicanism, Radicalism and Rebellion* (Dublin, 1993)

Dickson, William Steel, *Scripture Politics* (Belfast, 1812; repr., ed. Brendan Clifford, Belfast, 1991)

Doyle, David N., *Ireland, Irishmen and Revolutionary America, 1760–1820* (Dublin, 1981)

Duffy, Michael, *Soldiers, Sugar and Seapower: The British Expeditions to the West Indies and the War against Revolutionary France* (Oxford, 1987)

Durey, Michael, *Transatlantic Radicals and the Early American Republic* (Lawrence, Kans., 1997)

Elliott, Marianne, *Watchmen in Sion: The Protestant Idea of Liberty* (Derry, 1985)

—— *Wolfe Tone: Prophet of Independence* (New Haven, 1989)

McDowell, R. B., *Ireland in the Age of Imperialism and Revolution* (Oxford, 1979)

McNeill, Mary, *The Life and Times of Mary Ann McCracken, 1770–1866* (Belfast, 1988)

Pakenham, Thomas, *The Year of Liberty* (London, 1972)

Smyth, Jim, *The Men of No Property: Irish Radicals and Popular Politics in the Late Eighteenth Century* (London, 1992)

Stewart, A. T. Q., *A Deeper Silence: The Hidden Origins of the United Irishmen* (London, 1993)

—— *The Summer Soldiers: The 1798 Rebellion in Antrim and Down* (Belfast, 1995)

Young, Robert M., *Ulster in '98: Episodes and Anecdotes* (3rd ed., Belfast, 1893)

Index